Meat Cooking

Marks & Spencer
A dry red wine
from vineyards of the
Bordeaux region
Best served at room temperature

Meat
Cooking
Rosemary Wadey

Sundial

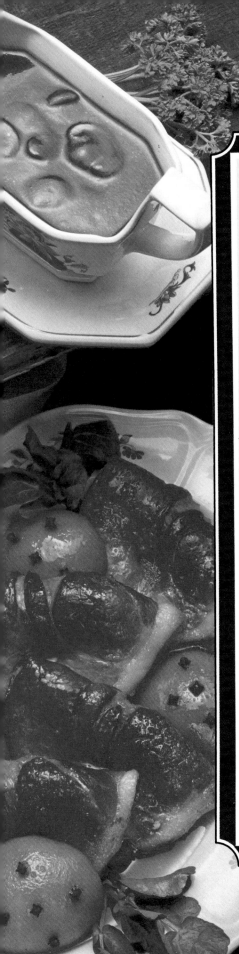

Contents

First published in 1977 by Sundial Books Limited
59 Grosvenor Street, London W1

© 1977 Hennerwood Publications Limited

ISBN 0 904230 41 4

Printed in England by Severn Valley Press Limited

Introduction

For many of us meat is the most important, satisfying and versatile of all foods. Meat supplies us with plenty of protein and is a good source of iron and some of the important B vitamins. The fat is an energy giver which also brings out much of the flavour of the meat and helps to keep the lean succulent during cooking.

The expensive cuts are usually taken from the tender part of the animal which has had the least amount of exercise; these include joints for roasting and steaks, chops and escalopes for grilling and frying. The tougher parts need longer, slower cooking, but they are just as nutritious as the prime cuts, have plenty of flavour and are often versatile.

As a general guide to buying, meat should not have an undue amount of fat on it – but it must have some. The fat should be firm and free from discoloration, and the lean should be firm with a fine grain and have no visible bruising.

Never store raw meat tightly wrapped in anything after purchase. It must be kept in the cold and have good air circulation. It is often best to put it on a plate, cover lightly but leave the ends open, and store in the refrigerator or a cold larder until required. Fresh meat should not be kept for more than 3–4 days even in the refrigerator, and minced raw meats and offal should be kept for only one day, because they are extremely perishable. Cooked meats should be wrapped in film or foil to prevent drying out; and leftover stews, casseroles, etc, must be cooled quickly before being covered and stored in the refrigerator until the next day. Remember reheated dishes must be completely heated through before serving again.

Here are a few general hints for roasting. Basically there are two methods. One is to use a hot oven (220°C, 425°F, Gas Mark 7) which quickly seals the outside of the joint and keeps the juices in. This gives a good meaty flavour and a well browned outside. The other is to use a moderately hot oven (190°C, 375°F, Gas Mark 5) which gives a moister joint with less shrinkage, but in my opinion not such a good flavour. The joint should be put into a roasting tin with the thickest layer of fat upwards so that it will automatically baste itself. Often dripping is spread over the meat. Take care not to prick the meat whilst cooking or you will lose many of the valuable juices. Basting with the hot dripping will help keep the joint moist.

Roasting of meat using roaster bags, film or foil is preferred by some people, but the meat remains pale in colour and doesn't develop such a good flavour as with open roasting. Suggested oven temperatures and cooking times are given on the packets and should be followed.
the best results.

Whatever method of roasting you choose the meat should be put in the centre of the oven after arranging the shelves correctly. When cooked the meat should be left to 'set' for a few minutes before carving.

Beef

When you buy beef, the lean should be a bright red and the fat a creamy yellow. Small flecks of fat should be visible throughout the lean.

Sirloin – boned and rolled, or on the bone. Roast.
Ribs – wing, corner, top. It can be on the bone or boned and rolled and is excellent for roasting; also suitable for pot roasting or braising.
Topside – usually boned and rolled. Pot roasting or braising gives best results.
Silverside – a boneless joint often salted. It needs long, slow cooking, such as boiling or braising.
Aitchbone – boned and rolled or left on bone. Roast, boil, braise. It is a little fatty on top.
Brisket – has excellent flavour but may be fatty. Needs long, slow cooking, braising, pot roasting or slow roasting.
Stewing meats – leg and shin need very long, slow cooking. Chuck and bladebone steak are suitable for casseroles, pies, etc.
Steaks – rump, fillet, entrecôte and other cuts can all be grilled or fried as you prefer.

Lamb

Age is indicated by the colour of the lean. Pale pink denotes young lamb and this turns to light red as the age increases. Home produced lamb is only available in the spring and early summer; imported lamb is available all the year.

Leg – often sold cut in half as it is a large and expensive joint. Suitable for roasting as well as making kebabs, casseroles, etc.
Shoulder – again can be cut in half, or boned, rolled and stuffed before roasting, good flavour.
Loin – very good for roasting either on the bone or boned, stuffed and rolled. Can also be pot roasted, cut into chops or made into noisettes.
Best end of neck – can be roasted or pot roasted in a joint, cut into cutlets to grill or fry. This cut is made into crown of lamb, guard of honour, etc.

Breast of lamb – this is a versatile, cheap and tasty cut. It is fatty. Can be boned, stuffed and rolled and roasted, casseroled or fried.

Middle and scrag end – stews, casseroles, hotpots.

Pork

Pork should have a good layer of firm white fat with a thick skin around the pale pink and moist lean. The skin should be scored for any joint to be roasted, to give crackling.

Leg – large lean joint often boned and rolled and cut into small joints, also good on the bone. Roast.

Loin – a prime roasting joint on or off the bone. Can also be cut into loin chops to grill, fry or casserole.

Spare rib – roast, but also good to braise or stew.

Boneless pork steaks or slices – usually taken from spare rib. Can be grilled, fried, casseroled, etc.

Fillet – a prime piece of meat with no fat. Also called tenderloin. Very versatile and excellent for kebabs, stroganoff and grilling or frying.

Blade – an economical cut. Roast, braise or stew.

Hand and spring – this is the foreleg and can be used for roasting, braising and stewing, or can be minced.

Belly – cheap, fatty but flavoursome. On or off the bone (stuffed and rolled). Roast or boil

American spare ribs – taken from the belly, they are really delicious and excellent for barbecuing.

Veal

Veal should come from a young calf; it should have a pale pink, fine meat which is soft and moist with very little firm pinkish or white fat.

Leg – a prime joint, boned, stuffed and rolled or on the bone, suitable for roasting.

Loin – prime cut for roasting, usually boned and rolled. Also cut into cutlets from the neck end and chops from the other, which can be fried, grilled, braised, etc.

Fillet – can be sold in a piece for roasting but is usually cut into escalopes.

Shoulder – often boned, rolled and roasted, also cut into pieces for pies, fricassées, casseroles, etc.

Knuckle – a cheap cut. Stew, braise or pot roast.

Breast – usually boned, stuffed, rolled and roasted.

Pie Veal – taken from the trimmings, it is boneless.

Bacon and Ham

Bacon is either sold as green or unsmoked bacon or goes through the process of smoking. Smoked bacon will keep the longer. The cuts of bacon vary in different parts of the country.

Back – lean prime rashers with a good 'eye' of meat and a distinct layer of fat. Can also be cut into thick chops to grill or fry, or bought as a piece to boil.

Streaky – narrow rashers, sometimes rather fat but with equal proportions of mixed fat and lean with a good flavour. Grilled, fried or boiled.

Collar – one of the best flavoured boiling, baking or braising joints. Provides meaty rashers.

Middle cut – this is a long rasher where the back and streaky are left joined together. A good joint when rolled, and can be stuffed to boil or roast.

Forehock – large inexpensive cut either on the bone or boned and rolled. Boil, roast, use for hotpot, or mince.

Gammon – the prime cut with little fat. Sold as a whole but is also cut into smaller joints with or without bone.

Sausages

The most popular sausages are pork or beef based. Pork are the more expensive and more delicately flavoured. Beef sausages are stronger.

Freezing

The casseroles and pies in this book are suitable for freezing, but undercook casseroles by half an hour. Cool very quickly and chill, then wrap securely in freezer foil or heavy-gauge polythene, or use plastic or wax containers for casseroles. Label clearly and freeze in the quick-freeze compartment. Store for 2–3 months only.

All spoon measurements are level.

All recipes serve four unless otherwise stated.

Marinaded brisket pot roast

Traditional roast beef

Metric

*Prime joint of beef on
bone, ie sirloin, ribs,
aitchbone ($1\frac{1}{4}$–$2\frac{3}{4}$ kg)
or a prime joint of beef,
boned and rolled, ie
sirloin, ribs, topside
25–50 g dripping
Salt and freshly ground
black pepper (optional)*

Yorkshire puddings:
*50 g plain flour
Pinch of salt
1 egg
150 ml milk
A little dripping*

Imperial

*Prime joint of beef on
bone, ie sirloin, ribs,
aitchbone ($2\frac{1}{2}$–6 lb)
or a prime joint of beef,
boned and rolled, ie
sirloin, ribs, topside
1–2 oz dripping
Salt and freshly ground
black pepper (optional)*

Yorkshire puddings:
*2 oz plain flour
Pinch of salt
1 egg
$\frac{1}{4}$ pint milk
A little dripping*

Cooking Time: depends on size.
Oven: 220°C, 425°F, Gas Mark 7.

Wipe the meat and trim if necessary. Weigh and calculate the cooking time required. For joints on the bone allow 20 minutes per 450 g (1 lb), plus 20 minutes over; for a boned and rolled joint allow 25 minutes per 450 g (1 lb), plus 25 minutes over; to give a medium cooked joint. For rare-cooked meat cut the cooking time by 5 minutes per 450 g (1 lb), and for a very well cooked joint add 5 minutes per 450 g (1 lb).

Place the joint in a roasting tin with the thickest layer of fat upwards. Cover with dripping and season lightly. Cook in a hot oven, basting several times, and roast potatoes alongside the joint. Serve with Yorkshire puddings, horseradish sauce and a thin gravy made using the pan juices.

Beef can also be roasted in a moderately hot oven (190°C, 375°F, Gas Mark 5), allowing 25 minutes per 450 g (1 lb), plus 25 minutes over, for meat on the bone; 30 minutes per 450 g (1 lb), plus 30 minutes over, for boned and rolled joints; to give medium cooked meat. Increase or decrease the times slightly for well cooked or rare meat.

To make Yorkshire puddings, sieve the flour with a pinch of salt into a bowl, add the egg and gradually beat in the milk to give a smooth batter. Add a little dripping to four individual Yorkshire pudding tins, or 10–12 patty tins, and put into an oven (220°C, 425°F, Gas Mark 7), until the fat is really hot. Pour in the batter and cook for 15 to 20 minutes until well puffed up and browned. To make one large pudding, use double the quantity and a 20 cm (8 inch) square tin, increase the cooking time to 35 to 40 minutes.

Marinaded brisket pot roast

Metric

1¼ kg lean brisket of beef,
boned and rolled
150 ml red wine
2 × 15 ml spoons dripping
8 small onions, peeled
4 carrots, peeled and
thickly sliced
4 sticks celery, scrubbed
and thickly sliced
10 whole cloves
2 bay leaves
Salt and freshly ground
black pepper
150 ml beef stock
1 × 15 ml spoon cornflour

Imperial

2½ lb lean brisket of beef,
boned and rolled
¼ pint red wine
2 tablespoons dripping
8 small onions, peeled
4 carrots, peeled and
thickly sliced
4 sticks celery, scrubbed
and thickly sliced
10 whole cloves
2 bay leaves
Salt and freshly ground
black pepper
¼ pint beef stock
1 tablespoon cornflour

Cooking Time: 3–4 hours for marinading, plus 3–3½ hours. Oven: 160°C, 325°F, Gas Mark 3.

Lay the joint in a deep dish. Pour over the wine and leave to marinade for 3–4 hours, turning several times. Remove and dry.

Fry the joint in hot dripping until well browned all over then place in a deep ovenproof casserole. Arrange the onions, carrots, celery, cloves and bay leaves around the meat. Season well and pour on the wine marinade and stock. Cover with a lid or foil and cook in a warm oven for 3–3½ hours or until tender.

Place the joint on a serving dish. Drain the vegetables and place in a dish. Strain the cooking liquor into a saucepan, skim off any fat and thicken with the cornflour blended in a little cold water. Bring to the boil for 2 minutes, taste and adjust the seasonings and serve with the joint.

Roast Beef

Beef and macaroni bake

Metric

225 g short-cut macaroni
Salt and freshly ground
black pepper
1 large onion, peeled
and sliced
1–2 cloves garlic, crushed
2 carrots, peeled
and chopped
1–2 × 15 ml spoons oil
450 g raw minced beef
150 ml stock
100 g mushrooms, cleaned,
trimmed and chopped
1 bay leaf
½ teaspoon Worcestershire
sauce
1 × 5 ml spoon oregano
25 g butter or margarine
25 g flour
300 ml milk
75 g English Mature
Cheddar cheese, grated
To garnish:
Tomato wedges

Imperial

8 oz short-cut macaroni
Salt and freshly ground
black pepper
1 large onion, peeled
and sliced
1–2 cloves garlic, crushed
2 carrots, peeled and
chopped
1–2 tablespoons oil
1 lb raw minced beef
¼ pint stock
4 oz mushrooms, cleaned,
trimmed and chopped
1 bay leaf
½ teaspoon Worcestershire
sauce
1 teaspoon oregano
1 oz butter or margarine
1 oz flour
½ pint milk
3 oz English Mature
Cheddar cheese, grated
To garnish:
Tomato wedges

Cooking Time: about 1 hour.
Oven: 200°C, 400°F, Gas Mark 6.

Cook the macaroni in plenty of boiling salted water, as directed on the packet, or until just tender. Drain.
Fry the onion, garlic and carrots in the oil until soft and lightly coloured. Add the mince and continue for 5 minutes, stirring frequently. Add the stock, mushrooms, bay leaf, Worcestershire sauce and seasonings, cover and simmer for 15 to 20 minutes. Discard the bay leaf. Taste and adjust the seasonings and stir in the oregano.
To make the sauce, melt the butter or margarine in a pan and stir in the flour. Cook for 1 minute then gradually add the milk and bring to the boil, stirring continuously. Simmer for 3 minutes, season to taste and stir in 50 g (2 oz) cheese until melted.
In a lightly greased ovenproof dish layer up one-third of the cooked macaroni followed by half the meat and half the sauce. Continue with half the macaroni, remaining meat, remaining macaroni and finally the sauce. Sprinkle with grated cheese and cook in a moderately hot oven for about 40 minutes until well browned.
Serve garnished with wedges of tomato.

Lasagne verdi

Metric

8–12 sheets lasagne verdi
Salt, and freshly ground
black pepper
2 × 15 ml spoons oil
1 onion, peeled and
finely chopped
2 sticks celery, scrubbed
and finely chopped
1 carrot, peeled and
finely chopped
1 clove garlic, crushed
350 g raw minced beef
226 g can peeled tomatoes
2 × 15 ml spoons tomato
purée
4 × 15 ml spoons red wine
1 × 5 ml spoon oregano
1 bay leaf

Béchamel sauce:
600 ml milk
Few slices raw onion
1 bay leaf
40 g butter
40 g flour
25–50 g cheese, grated
1 × 15 ml spoon Parmesan
cheese, grated

Imperial

8–12 sheets lasagne verdi
Salt, and freshly ground
black pepper
2 tablespoons oil
1 onion, peeled and
finely chopped
2 sticks celery, scrubbed
and finely chopped
1 carrot, peeled and
finely chopped
1 clove garlic, crushed
12 oz raw minced beef
8 oz can peeled tomatoes
2 tablespoons tomato
purée
4 tablespoons red wine
1 teaspoon oregano
1 bay leaf

Béchamel sauce:
1 pint milk
Few slices raw onion
1 bay leaf
1½ oz butter
1½ oz flour
1–2 oz cheese, grated
1 tablespoon Parmesan
cheese, grated

Cooking Time: about 1½ hours.
Oven: 200°C, 400°F, Gas Mark 6.

Cook the lasagne in boiling salted water with 1 × 15 ml spoon (1 tablespoon) oil added, following the directions on the packet. Drain on absorbent kitchen paper.
Fry the onion, celery, carrot and garlic in the remaining oil for 5 minutes. Stir in the mince and cook for a further 5 minutes, stirring frequently. Add the tomatoes, tomato purée, wine, seasonings, oregano and bay leaf, cover and simmer for about 40 minutes, stirring occasionally and adding a little more liquid if necessary.
Meanwhile, to make the Béchamel sauce, place the milk in a pan with the onion and bay leaf, bring slowly to the boil and leave to cool. Melt the butter in a pan, stir in the flour and cook for 1 minute. Strain the infused milk and gradually add to the roux, stirring continuously until boiling. Simmer for 2 minutes then taste and adjust the seasonings. Use the lasagne to line a lightly greased ovenproof dish about 5 cm (2 in) deep. Spread with a layer of meat sauce and then a layer of Béchamel sauce. Continue to layer the lasagne and sauces until used up, finishing with a layer of Béchamel sauce.
Sprinkle with a mixture of Cheddar and Parmesan cheese and cook in a moderately hot oven for about 25 minutes until golden brown and bubbling.

Lasagne verdi; Beef and macaroni bake; Chilli con carne

Chilli con carne

Metric

450 g raw minced beef
2 large onions, peeled
and thinly sliced
1–2 × 5 ml spoons chilli
powder
Salt and freshly ground
black pepper
Paprika
822 g can peeled tomatoes
454 g can red kidney
beans, drained

Imperial

1 lb raw minced beef
2 large onions, peeled
and thinly sliced
1–2 teaspoons chilli powder
Salt and freshly ground
black pepper
Paprika
1 lb 13 oz can peeled
tomatoes
16 oz can red kidney
beans, drained

Cooking Time: 1¾–2 hours.

Fry the mince slowly in a non-stick pan for about 10 minutes, stirring frequently. Add the onion and chilli powder and cook gently for a further 5 minutes. Season well with salt, lightly with pepper and paprika, add the canned tomatoes and bring to the boil. Cover and simmer very gently for 1–1¼ hours, adding a little boiling water during cooking, if necessary, and stirring occasionally.

Add the beans, taste and adjust the seasonings and continue for a further 15 to 20 minutes.

Serve in earthenware bowls and eat with a spoon with lots of hot crusty bread.

Beef and horseradish pasties; Curried beef loaf; Curried meatballs

Curried meatballs

Metric

450 g raw minced beef
1 onion, peeled and finely chopped
1 × 15 ml spoon curry powder
Salt and freshly ground black pepper
1 × 5 ml spoon Worcestershire sauce
75 g sultanas
25 g fresh breadcrumbs
1 egg, beaten
Flour for coating
Fat for frying
1 onion, peeled and finely sliced
2 carrots, peeled and diced
15 g flour
2 × 5 ml spoons tomato purée
450 ml beef stock

Imperial

1 lb raw minced beef
1 onion, peeled and finely chopped
1 tablespoon curry powder
Salt and freshly ground black pepper
1 teaspoon Worcestershire sauce
3 oz sultanas
1 oz fresh breadcrumbs
1 egg, beaten
Flour for coating
Fat for frying
1 onion, peeled and finely sliced
2 carrots, peeled and diced
½ oz flour
2 teaspoons tomato purée
¾ pint beef stock

Cooking Time: about 1 hour.
Oven: 180°C, 350°F, Gas Mark 4.

Mix together the mince, onion, 1 × 5 ml spoon (1 teaspoon) of the curry powder, the seasonings, Worcestershire sauce, 25 g (1 oz) of the sultanas and the breadcrumbs and bind together with the egg. Divide into 16 and shape into balls then coat in flour. Fry in a little fat until browned all over then transfer to an ovenproof casserole.

Retain 1 × 15 ml spoon (1 tablespoon) fat in the pan and fry the onion and carrots until lightly coloured. Stir in the remaining curry powder, flour and tomato purée and cook for 1 to 2 minutes. Gradually add the stock and bring to the boil. Season, add the remaining sultanas and pour over the meatballs. Cover and cook in a moderate oven for about 45 minutes, or until tender.

Taste, adjust the seasonings and serve the meatballs with freshly boiled rice.

Curried beef loaf

Metric

350 g raw minced beef
Salt and freshly ground
black pepper
2 × 5 ml spoons curry
powder
2 × 15 ml spoons mango
chutney
1 onion, peeled and
finely chopped
50 g fresh breadcrumbs
1 large egg, beaten

Sauce:
1 medium-sized onion,
peeled and chopped
50 g butter or margarine
1–2 × 5 ml spoons curry
powder
40 g flour
450 ml stock
2 × 15 ml spoons chopped
gherkins

Imperial

12 oz raw minced beef
Salt and freshly ground
black pepper
2 teaspoons curry powder
2 tablespoons mango
chutney
1 onion, peeled and
finely chopped
2 oz fresh breadcrumbs
1 large egg, beaten

Sauce:
1 medium-sized onion,
peeled and chopped
2 oz butter or margarine
1–2 teaspoons curry
powder
1½ oz flour
¾ pint stock
2 tablespoons chopped
gherkins

Cooking Time: 1½–1¾ hours.
Oven: 160°C, 325°F, Gas Mark 3.

Mix the mince with plenty of seasonings, the curry powder, chutney, onion and breadcrumbs and bind together with the egg. Turn into a well greased 450 g (1 lb) loaf tin and press well down. Stand in a baking tin containing 4 cm (1½ inches) water and cook in a warm oven for 1½–1¾ hours until firm to the touch and cooked through.

Meanwhile, to make the sauce, fry the onion in butter until soft then stir in the curry powder and flour. Cook for 1 minute then gradually add the stock and bring to the boil for 2 minutes. Season to taste and stir in the gherkins.

Turn the loaf out on to a serving dish and serve with the hot sauce. Garnish with gherkins, if liked.

Beef and horseradish pasties

Metric

225 g raw minced beef
1 onion, peeled and finely
chopped
50 g raw potato, peeled
and finely chopped
1 carrot, peeled and
coarsely grated
Salt and freshly ground
black pepper
1 × 15 ml spoon creamed
horseradish

Pastry:
200 g plain flour
Pinch of salt
50 g margarine
50 g lard or white fat
Water to mix
Beaten egg or milk to
glaze

Imperial

8 oz raw minced beef
1 onion, peeled and finely
chopped
2 oz raw potato, peeled
and finely chopped
1 carrot, peeled and
coarsely grated
Salt and freshly ground
black pepper
1 tablespoon creamed
horseradish

Pastry:
8 oz plain flour
Pinch of salt
2 oz margarine
2 oz lard or white fat
Water to mix
Beaten egg or milk to
glaze

Cooking Time: 45 minutes
Oven: 220°C, 425°F, Gas Mark 7
180°C, 350°F, Gas Mark 4.

Mix the mince with the onion, potato, carrot, plenty of seasonings and the horseradish.

To make the pastry, sieve the flour with a pinch of salt into a bowl. Add the fats and rub in until the mixture resembles fine breadcrumbs. Add sufficient water to mix to a pliable dough. Roll out two-thirds of the pastry on a floured surface and use to line four individual Yorkshire pudding tins. Fill with the meat mixture and cover with pastry lids, dampened around the edges. Press the edges well together and crimp. Decorate the tops with the pastry trimmings. Brush with egg or milk and cook in a hot oven for 15 minutes. Reduce oven temperature to moderate and continue for 25 to 30 minutes until golden brown. Serve hot.

Spiced silverside

Metric	Imperial
1½–1¾ kg piece of salted silverside	3–3½ lb piece of salted silverside
2 onions, peeled and sliced, or 8 button onions, peeled	2 onions, peeled and sliced, or 8 button onions, peeled
1 leek, trimmed, sliced and washed	1 leek, trimmed, sliced and washed
4 large carrots, peeled and halved	4 large carrots, peeled and halved
2 sticks celery, scrubbed and sliced	2 sticks celery, scrubbed and sliced
2 bay leaves	2 bay leaves
8–12 whole cloves	8–12 whole cloves
50 g soft brown sugar	2 oz soft brown sugar
½ teaspoon ground cinnamon	½ teaspoon ground cinnamon
½ teaspoon dry mustard	½ teaspoon dry mustard
2 × 15 ml spoons orange juice	2 tablespoons orange juice

Cooking Time: about 3¼ hours.
Oven: 180°C, 350°F, Gas Mark 4.

Place the joint in a saucepan with the vegetables and bay leaves and cover with water. Bring to the boil, remove the scum, then cover and simmer gently for about 2½ hours. Allow to cool slightly in the liquor then drain and place in a roasting tin.

Stud the fat with the cloves. Mix together the sugar, cinnamon, mustard, and orange juice and spread over the meat. Cook in a moderate oven for 30 minutes or until tender, basting occasionally. Remove and keep warm, place the vegetables around the joint.

Stir 450 ml (¾ pint) of the cooking liquor into the pan drippings and bring to the boil for 3 minutes. Season to taste and serve with the joint.

Paprika mince

Metric	Imperial
1 large onion, peeled and sliced	1 large onion, peeled and sliced
1 clove garlic, crushed	1 clove garlic, crushed
1 × 15 ml spoon dripping or oil	1 tablespoon dripping or oil
450 g raw minced beef	1 lb raw minced beef
1 × 15 ml spoon flour	1 tablespoon flour
1 × 15 ml spoon paprika	1 tablespoon paprika
1 × 15 ml spoon tomato purée	1 tablespoon tomato purée
4 tomatoes, peeled and quartered	4 tomatoes, peeled and quartered
Salt and freshly ground black pepper	Salt and freshly ground black pepper
150 ml stock	¼ pint stock
1 × 15 ml spoon wine vinegar	1 tablespoon wine vinegar
½ teaspoon caraway seeds (optional)	½ teaspoon caraway seeds (optional)

To garnish:
150 ml soured cream
Finely chopped parsley

To garnish:
¼ pint soured cream
Finely chopped parsley

Cooking Time: 1¼ hours.
Oven: 160°C, 325°F, Gas Mark 3.

Fry the onion and garlic in the dripping or oil until lightly browned. Stir in the mince and cook gently for about 5 minutes, stirring frequently. Add the flour, paprika, tomato paste, tomatoes, seasonings, stock, vinegar and caraway seeds (if using). Bring to the boil, transfer to an ovenproof casserole, cover and cook in a warm oven for 1 hour.

Spoon the soured cream over the meat and sprinkle with parsley. Serve with boiled noodles.

Paprika mince; Spiced silverside; Cabbage dolmades

Cabbage dolmades

Metric

25 g butter
1 onion, peeled and chopped
4 rashers streaky bacon derinded and chopped
225 g raw minced beef
50 g long grain rice, cooked
25 g olives, chopped
4 × 5 ml spoons soy sauce
Salt and freshly ground black pepper
12 large cabbage leaves
300 ml seasoned boiling stock
1 × 15 ml spoon cornflour
2 × 5 ml spoons tomato purée

Imperial

1 oz butter
1 onion, peeled and chopped
4 rashers streaky bacon, derinded and chopped
8 oz raw minced beef
2 oz long grain rice, cooked
1 oz olives, chopped
4 teaspoons soy sauce
Salt and freshly ground black pepper
12 large cabbage leaves
½ pint seasoned boiling stock
1 tablespoon cornflour
2 teaspoons tomato purée

Cooking Time: about 1 hour.
Oven: 160°C, 325°F, Gas Mark 3.

Melt the butter in a pan and fry the onion and bacon until lightly coloured. Stir in the mince and cook for 5 minutes, stirring frequently. Stir in the cooked rice, olives, 3 × 5 ml spoons (3 teaspoons) of the soy sauce and the seasonings. Blanch the cabbage leaves in boiling salted water for 3 minutes, then drain. Divide the mixture between the cabbage leaves and roll up to enclose the filling. Place in a lightly greased ovenproof casserole and pour over the boiling stock. Cover the casserole and cook in a warm oven for 40 minutes.

Strain off the cooking liquor into a small pan. Add the cornflour blended in a little cold water, the tomato purée and the remaining soy sauce and bring to the boil for 2 minutes. Taste and adjust the seasonings. Pour back over the dolmades.

Cidered beef with dumplings

Metric

550 g braising steak
A little seasoned flour
2 × 15 ml spoons
dripping or lard
1 large onion, peeled and
chopped
3 sticks celery, scrubbed
and sliced
300 ml dry cider
300 ml beef stock
Salt and freshly ground
black pepper

Dumplings:
100 g self-raising flour
Pinch of salt
50 g shredded suet
1 × 5 ml spoon mixed
herbs
Water to mix

Imperial

1¼ lb braising steak
A little seasoned flour
2 tablespoons dripping or
lard
1 large onion, peeled and
chopped
3 sticks celery, scrubbed
and sliced
½ pint dry cider
½ pint beef stock
Salt and freshly ground
black pepper

Dumplings:
4 oz self-raising flour
Pinch of salt
2 oz shredded suet
1 teaspoon mixed herbs
Water to mix

Cooking Time: about 2 hours.
Oven: 160°C, 325°F, Gas Mark 3.

Trim the beef and cut into 2·5 cm (1 in) cubes. Toss in seasoned flour. Melt the fat and fry the meat until well browned then transfer to an ovenproof casserole.

Fry the onion and celery gently for a few minutes in the same fat then stir in 1 × 15 ml spoon (1 tablespoon) seasoned flour and cook for 1 minute. Add the cider and stock and bring to the boil. Season to taste and pour over the beef. Cover and cook in a warm oven for 1½ hours, or until the meat is almost tender.

Meanwhile, to make the dumplings, mix together the flour, a pinch of salt, suet and herbs and mix to a soft dough with water. Form into 8 balls. Add to the casserole and continue cooking for a further 20 to 30 minutes or until the dumplings are cooked.

Taste and adjust the seasonings before serving.

Boeuf bourguignonne; Beef and chestnut pie

Cidered beef with dumplings

Boeuf bourguignonne

Metric	Imperial
675 g topside of beef	1½ lb topside of beef
200 ml red wine	7 fl oz red wine
1 clove garlic, crushed	1 clove garlic, crushed
1 bay leaf	1 bay leaf
25 g dripping or lard	1 oz dripping or lard
100 g streaky bacon, derinded and diced	4 oz streaky bacon, derinded and diced
12 button onions, peeled	12 button onions, peeled
1 × 15 ml spoon flour	1 tablespoon flour
200 ml beef stock	7 fl oz beef stock
Salt and freshly ground black pepper	Salt and freshly ground black pepper
2–3 × 15 ml spoons brandy (optional)	2–3 tablespoons brandy (optional)
100 g button mushrooms, cleaned and trimmed	4 oz button mushrooms, cleaned and trimmed

Cooking Time: several hours for marinading, plus 2–2½ hours. Oven: 160°C, 325°F, Gas Mark 3.

Trim the meat and cut into 2·5 cm (1 in) cubes. Place in a bowl with the wine, garlic and bay leaf; cover and leave for several hours, or overnight, in a cold place.
Drain the meat thoroughly. Melt the fat in a pan and fry the meat quickly until well browned all over. Transfer to an ovenproof casserole. Fry the bacon and onions until lightly browned and transfer to the casserole. Stir the flour into the fat in the pan and cook for 1 minute then gradually add the wine marinade and stock and bring to the boil. Season to taste and pour into the casserole. Cover and cook in a warm oven for 1½ hours. Warm the brandy (if using), ignite and add to the casserole with the mushrooms. Return to the oven for 15 to 30 minutes until tender. Discard the bay leaf, taste and adjust the seasonings before serving. A little extra stock may be required.

Beef and chestnut pie

Metric	Imperial
550 g braising steak	1¼ lb braising steak
25 g butter	1 oz butter
1 × 15 ml spoon oil	1 tablespoon oil
12 button onions, peeled	12 button onions, peeled
2 × 15 ml spoons flour	2 tablespoons flour
450 ml beef stock	¾ pint beef stock
4 × 15 ml spoons wine	4 tablespoons wine
Salt and freshly ground black pepper	Salt, and freshly ground black pepper
225 g chestnuts, lightly roasted and peeled	8 oz chestnuts, lightly roasted and peeled
Pastry:	Pastry:
160 g plain flour	6 oz plain flour
Pinch of salt	Pinch of salt
40 g margarine	1½ oz margarine
40 g lard or white fat	1½ oz lard or white fat
Water to mix	Water to mix
Beaten egg or milk	Beaten egg or milk

Cooking Time: about 2¼ hours.
Oven: 180°C, 350°F, Gas Mark 4.
220°C, 425°F, Gas Mark 7.

Trim the meat and cut into 2·5 cm (1 in) cubes. Fry in butter and oil until well browned. Transfer to an ovenproof casserole. Fry the onions until lightly browned and add to the casserole. Stir the flour into the pan, cook for 1 minute, gradually add stock and wine, bring to the boil. Season well, add the chestnuts and pour over the beef. Cover and cook in a moderate oven for about 1¼ hours, until tender. Pour into a pie dish and leave to cool.
To make the pastry, sieve the flour with a pinch of salt, add the fats and rub in until the mixture resembles fine crumbs. Add enough water to mix. Roll out slightly larger than the top of the dish and cut a 2·5 cm (1 in) wide strip all round. Place the strip on the wetted rim of the dish, brush with water. Position the lid. Trim edges, crimp and decorate with pastry trimmings. Brush with egg or milk and cook in a hot oven for 15 minutes. Continue in a moderate oven for 25 to 30 minutes, until pastry is cooked.

Beery beef

Metric

675 g chuck or braising
steak, in one piece
3 × 15 ml spoons flour
Salt and freshly ground
black pepper
2 × 15 ml spoons dripping
2 large onions, peeled
and thinly sliced
1 clove garlic, crushed
300 ml brown ale
200 ml beef stock
2 large carrots, peeled
and sliced
¼ teaspoon ground nutmeg
1 × 5 ml spoon caster
sugar
2 × 5 ml spoons tomato
purée
1 × 5 ml spoon vinegar
1 bay leaf
100 g tiny button
mushrooms, cleaned and
trimmed

Imperial

1½ lb chuck or braising
steak, in one piece
3 tablespoons flour
Salt and freshly ground
black pepper
2 tablespoons dripping
2 large onions, peeled
and thinly sliced
1 clove garlic, crushed
½ pint brown ale
7 fl oz beef stock
2 large carrots, peeled
and sliced
¼ teaspoon ground nutmeg
1 teaspoon caster sugar
2 teaspoons tomato purée
1 teaspoon vinegar
1 bay leaf
4 oz tiny button
mushrooms, cleaned and
trimmed

Cooking Time: 2–2½ hours.
Oven: 160°C, 325°F, Gas Mark 3.

Trim the meat and cut into four or eight even-sized pieces.
Combine the flour with plenty of seasonings and use to
coat the meat. Heat the dripping in a pan and fry the meat
quickly until sealed all over. Transfer to an ovenproof
casserole.

Fry the onions and garlic in the same fat until golden brown
then stir in the remaining flour and cook for 1 minute.
Gradually stir in the ale and stock and bring to the boil.
Add all the remaining ingredients except the mushrooms
and pour over the meat. Cover casserole tightly and cook
in a warm oven for 1½ hours.

Add the mushrooms, taste and adjust seasonings, and
continue to cook for a further ½ to 1 hour, until very tender.
Turn on to a serving dish, and garnish with a parsley sprig,
if liked.

Beery beef

Oxtail provençale

Metric

1 large oxtail, cut up
Seasoned flour
2 × 15 ml spoons oil
2 onions, peeled and sliced
1–2 cloves garlic, crushed
2 large carrots, peeled
and sliced
2 sticks celery, scrubbed
and sliced
396 g can peeled tomatoes
1 × 15 ml spoon tomato
purée
600 ml stock
2 × 5 ml spoons oregano
Salt and freshly ground
black pepper
12 black olives

Imperial

1 large oxtail, cut up
Seasoned flour
2 tablespoons oil
2 onions, peeled and sliced
1–2 cloves garlic, crushed
2 large carrots, peeled
and sliced
2 sticks celery, scrubbed
and sliced
14 oz can peeled tomatoes
1 tablespoon tomato
purée
1 pint stock
2 teaspoons oregano
Salt and freshly ground
black pepper
12 black olives

Cooking Time: 4¼ hours.
Oven: 160°C, 325°F, Gas Mark 3.

Trim the oxtail of excess fat and coat the pieces in seasoned flour. Fry in the oil until evenly browned all over. Transfer to a large ovenproof casserole.

Fry the onions and garlic in the same oil until lightly coloured then add to the casserole with the carrots, celery, tomatoes, tomato purée, stock, oregano and plenty of seasonings. Cover tightly and cook in a warm oven for 3 hours.

If possible, cool and chill overnight in order to remove the layer of fat easily. If not, spoon off all the fat from the surface before continuing. Add the olives, taste and adjust the seasonings and return the casserole to the oven for another hour before serving.

Oxtail provençale

Cornish pie

Metric	Imperial
450 g raw minced beef	1 lb raw minced beef
175 g raw potato, peeled and finely chopped	6 oz raw potato, peeled and finely chopped
2 carrots, peeled and finely chopped	2 carrots, peeled and finely chopped
1 large onion, peeled and finely chopped	1 large onion, peeled and finely chopped
1 × 5 ml spoon mixed herbs	1 teaspoon mixed herbs
Salt and freshly ground black pepper	Salt and freshly ground black pepper
Pinch of ground nutmeg	Pinch of ground nutmeg

Pastry:	Pastry:
300 g plain flour	12 oz plain flour
Pinch of salt	Pinch of salt
75 g margarine	3 oz margarine
75 g lard or white fat	3 oz lard or white fat
Water to mix	Water to mix
Beaten egg or milk to glaze	Beaten egg or milk to glaze

Cooking Time: about 1 hour.
Oven: 220°C, 425°F, Gas Mark 7.
       180°C, 350°F, Gas Mark 4.

Mix together the mince, potato, carrots, onion and herbs and season the mixture very well with salt, pepper and nutmeg.

To make the pastry, sieve the flour into a bowl with a pinch of salt, add the fats and rub in until the mixture resembles fine breadcrumbs. Add sufficient water to mix to a pliable dough. Knead lightly then roll out two-thirds of the pastry on a floured surface to fit an oblong tin approx 28 × 18 × 4 cm (11 × 7 × 1½ in) deep.

Add the filling, pressing it down evenly. Roll out the remaining pastry to make a lid, damp the edges, place on pie and press the edges well together. Trim off the surplus pastry and crimp the edges. Use the pastry trimmings to decorate the top.

Brush with egg or milk and cook in a hot oven for 20 to 25 minutes, until beginning to brown; then reduce oven temperature to moderate and continue for a further 35 to 40 minutes.

Serve hot or cold.

Beef olives with walnuts

Metric	Imperial
1 onion, peeled and finely chopped	1 onion, peeled and finely chopped
4 rashers streaky bacon, derinded and chopped	4 rashers streaky bacon, derinded and chopped
1 clove garlic, crushed	1 clove garlic, crushed
25 g butter	1 oz butter
75 g fresh breadcrumbs	3 oz fresh breadcrumbs
50 g shelled walnuts, roughly chopped	2 oz shelled walnuts, roughly chopped
1 × 15 ml spoon finely chopped parsley	1 tablespoon finely chopped parsley
Salt and freshly ground black pepper	Salt and freshly ground black pepper
1 large egg, beaten	1 large egg, beaten
4 slices topside of beef, beaten flat	4 slices topside of beef, beaten flat
2 × 15 ml spoons oil	2 tablespoons oil
25 g flour	1 oz flour
450 ml beef stock	¾ pint beef stock
2–3 × 15 ml spoons dry sherry or white wine	2–3 tablespoons dry sherry or white wine

To garnish:	To garnish:
Few walnut halves	Few walnut halves
Parsley sprigs	Parsley sprigs

Cooking Time: 1½ hours.
Oven: 160°C, 325°F, Gas Mark 3.

Fry the onion, bacon and garlic in melted butter until lightly browned. Stir in the breadcrumbs, walnuts, parsley and seasonings and bind together with the egg. Divide into four and put one portion on each beef slice. Roll up beef slices to enclose the fillings and then secure with wooden cocktail sticks.

Fry in the heated oil until browned all over then transfer the olives to an ovenproof casserole. Stir the flour into the pan drippings and cook for 1 minute then gradually add the stock and sherry and bring to the boil. Season well and pour over the olives. Cover and cook in a warm oven for about 1¼ hours, or until tender.

Skim off any fat from the surface, taste and adjust the seasonings. Garnish with the walnut halves and parsley sprigs before serving.

Steak, kidney and aubergine pie; Beef olives with walnuts; Cornish pie

Steak, kidney and aubergine pie

Metric

450 g lean chuck steak
100 g kidney
2 × 15 ml spoons dripping
1 onion, peeled and
chopped
25 g flour
300 ml beef stock
Salt and freshly ground
black pepper
2 large tomatoes, peeled
and sliced
1 medium-sized
aubergine, washed and
cut into cubes
100 g mushrooms, cleaned
and trimmed
225 g puff pastry
Beaten egg to glaze

Imperial

1 lb lean chuck steak
4 oz kidney
2 tablespoons dripping
1 onion, peeled and
chopped
1 oz flour
½ pint beef stock
Salt and freshly ground
black pepper
2 large tomatoes, peeled
and sliced
1 medium-sized
aubergine, washed and
cut into cubes
4 oz mushrooms, cleaned
and trimmed
8 oz puff pastry
Beaten egg to glaze

Cooking Time: about 2¼ hours.
Oven: 180°C, 350°F, Gas Mark 4.
230°C, 450°F, Gas Mark 8.

Trim the beef and cut into 2·5 cm (1 in) cubes. Trim the kidney and cut into small pieces. Fry beef and kidney pieces in melted dripping until browned and well sealed. Transfer to an ovenproof casserole.

Fry the onion in the same fat until well browned then stir in the flour and cook for 1 minute. Gradually add the stock and bring to the boil for 2 minutes. Season well, add the tomatoes and pour into the casserole. Cover and cook in a moderate oven for 1 hour.

Add the aubergine and mushrooms and continue for a further ½ hour or until tender. Pour into a pie dish with a funnel in the centre and cool.

Raise oven temperature to very hot. Roll out the pastry, cut a 2·5 cm (1 in) strip and place on the dampened rim of the pie dish. Brush this strip with water then place on the pastry lid. Decorate with pastry trimmings, brush with egg and cook in the oven for about 30 minutes, until well risen and golden brown.

Beef and parsnip pie; Chunky burgers with piquant dressing; Beef croquettes with quick béarnaise sauce

Beef and parsnip pie

Metric

1 large onion, peeled
and chopped
1 clove garlic, crushed
2 sticks celery, scrubbed
and chopped
1 × 15 ml spoon dripping
450 g raw minced beef
1 × 15 ml spoon flour
1 × 15 ml spoon tomato
purée
150 ml stock
Salt and freshly ground
black pepper
1 × 5 ml spoon basil
350 g potatoes, peeled
and boiled
450 g parsnips, peeled
and boiled
40–50 g butter

Imperial

1 large onion, peeled
and chopped
1 clove garlic, crushed
2 sticks celery, scrubbed
and chopped
1 tablespoon dripping
1 lb raw minced beef
1 tablespoon flour
1 tablespoon tomato
purée
¼ pint stock
Salt and freshly ground
black pepper
1 teaspoon basil
12 oz potatoes, peeled
and boiled
1 lb parsnips, peeled
and boiled
1½–2 oz butter

Cooking Time: 1–1¼ hours.
Oven: 200°C, 400°F, Gas Mark 6.

Fry the onion, garlic and celery in the melted dripping until soft. Add the mince and cook gently for 10 minutes, stirring occasionally. Stir in the flour and tomato purée and then the stock, seasonings and herbs. Bring to the boil, cover and simmer gently for 15 to 20 minutes. Taste and adjust seasonings. Turn into an ovenproof dish.

Meanwhile mash the potatoes and parsnips together, add butter and seasonings to taste and beat until smooth. Either spread or pipe over the meat. Cook in moderately hot oven for 30 to 40 minutes until the top is browning.

Note: use a large plain vegetable nozzle for piping. Instant potato mash may be used in place of boiled potatoes.

Chunky burgers with piquant dressing

Metric

450 g raw minced beef
40 g fresh breadcrumbs
Salt and freshly ground
black pepper
¼ teaspoon ground mace
1 × 15 ml spoon finely
chopped parsley
4 × 15 ml spoons Tomato
Pickle (or other chunky
pickle)
1 egg, beaten
Flour for coating
Oil or dripping for frying

Dressing:
4 × 15 ml spoons thick
mayonnaise
2 × 15 ml spoons Tomato
Pickle
2 × 5 ml spoons lemon
juice
¼ teaspoon finely
grated lemon rind

To garnish:
Chicory spears
Coarsely grated carrot

Imperial

1 lb raw minced beef
1½ oz fresh breadcrumbs
Salt and freshly ground
black pepper
¼ teaspoon ground mace
1 tablespoon finely
chopped parsley
4 tablespoons Tomato
Pickle (or other chunky
pickle)
1 egg, beaten
Flour for coating
Oil or dripping for frying

Dressing:
4 tablespoons thick
mayonnaise
2 tablespoons Tomato
Pickle
2 teaspoons lemon juice
¼ teaspoon finely grated
lemon rind

To garnish:
Chicory spears
Coarsely grated carrot

Cooking Time: about 30 minutes.

Mix the beef with the breadcrumbs, seasonings, mace, parsley and pickle and bind together with the egg. Divide into four and shape into round flat cakes. (For smaller burgers divide the mixture into eight.) Coat evenly with flour. Fry in hot shallow fat for about 10 minutes each side until well browned and cooked through. Drain on absorbent kitchen paper and keep warm.

To make the dressing, mix together all the ingredients and season to taste.

Serve garnished with chicory and coarsely grated carrot.

Beef croquettes with quick béarnaise sauce

Metric

6 spring onions, cleaned,
trimmed, finely chopped
2 rashers lean bacon,
derinded and chopped
40 g butter
25 g flour
150 ml beef stock
225 g cooked beef, minced
1 × 15 ml spoon finely
chopped parsley
Salt and freshly ground
black pepper
2 eggs, beaten
100 g fresh breadcrumbs
Oil or fat for deep frying

Sauce:
6 × 15 ml spoons thick
mayonnaise
2 × 5 ml spoons tarragon
vinegar
2 spring onions, cleaned,
trimmed, finely chopped
1 × 5 ml spoon chopped
tarragon, fresh or dried

To garnish:
Parsley sprig

Imperial

6 spring onions, cleaned,
trimmed, finely chopped
2 rashers lean bacon,
derinded and chopped
1½ oz butter
1 oz flour
¼ pint beef stock
8 oz cooked beef, minced
1 tablespoon finely
chopped parsley
Salt and freshly ground
black pepper
2 eggs, beaten
4 oz fresh breadcrumbs
Oil or fat for deep frying

Sauce:
6 tablespoons thick
mayonnaise
2 teaspoons tarragon
vinegar
2 spring onions, cleaned,
trimmed, finely chopped
1 teaspoon chopped
tarragon, fresh or dried

To garnish:
Parsley sprig

Cooking Time: about 30 minutes.

Fry the onions and bacon gently in the melted butter until soft and lightly coloured. Stir in the flour and cook gently until pale brown. Gradually add the stock and bring to the boil, stirring continuously. Simmer for 2 minutes then remove from the heat and stir in the beef, parsley and seasonings to taste. Cool.

Divide into eight and shape into barrels on a floured surface. Dip into, or brush with, egg then coat in breadcrumbs; repeat this process again pressing well in. Chill until required.

To make the sauce, blend all the ingredients together, season to taste and place in a sauce boat.

Heat deep fat to 190°C/375°F, or until a cube of bread browns in 20 seconds, and fry the croquettes for 4 to 5 minutes until well browned and cooked through. Drain on absorbent kitchen paper, garnish with a parsley sprig and serve hot with the sauce.

Roast lamb

Metric	Imperial
Prime joint of lamb, ie, leg, shoulder, loin or best end of neck	Prime joint of lamb, ie, leg, shoulder, loin or best end of neck
25 g dripping	1 oz dripping
Salt and freshly ground black pepper	Salt and freshly ground black pepper

Optional flavourings:	Optional flavourings:
Crushed garlic	Crushed garlic
Fresh rosemary or other herbs	Fresh rosemary or other herbs

Cooking Time: depends on size of joint.
Oven: 220°C, 425°F, Gas Mark 7.

Trim the meat if necessary and weigh. The joints can either be cooked on the bone or boned and rolled, as you prefer. Often lamb is stuffed before roasting – in which case weigh after stuffing. Allow 20 minutes per 450 g (1 lb), plus 20 minutes over, for meat on the bone; 25 minutes per 450 g (1 lb), plus 25 minutes over, when boned and rolled.
Place joint in a roasting tin with the thickest layer of fat upwards and spread lightly with dripping. Season and rub with garlic and make slits and insert sprigs of rosemary (if using). Cook in a hot oven for the calculated time, basting several times. Serve lamb to taste, either slightly pink or well done, with a slightly thickened gravy made from the pan juices, and with roast potatoes, peas or a green vegetable and mint sauce.
Lamb can be roasted in a moderate oven (189°C, 350°F, Gas Mark 4), allowing 30–35 minutes per 450 g (1 lb) for joints on the bone, 40–45 minutes for boned and rolled joints. Specially prepared joints such as Crown of Lamb, Guards of Honour, etc, are usually cooked in a moderate oven.

Roast crown of lamb

Metric	Imperial
2 best ends of neck of lamb (12 cutlets) or a crown of lamb	2 best ends of neck of lamb (12 cutlets) or a crown of lamb
little oil	little oil

Stuffing:	Stuffing:
25 g butter	1 oz butter
1 large onion, peeled and finely chopped	1 large onion, peeled and finely chopped
2 sticks celery, scrubbed and finely chopped	2 sticks celery, scrubbed and finely chopped
100 g brown breadcrumbs	4 oz brown breadcrumbs
Pinch of garlic powder	Pinch of garlic powder
Salt and freshly ground black pepper	Salt and freshly ground black pepper
50 g salted peanuts, chopped	2 oz salted peanuts, chopped
75 g long-grain rice, cooked	3 oz long-grain rice, cooked
1 × 5 ml spoon curry powder	1 level teaspoon curry powder
1 large egg, beaten	1 large egg, beaten

To garnish:	To garnish:
Freshly cooked peas	Freshly cooked peas
Cooked whole baby carrots	Cooked whole baby carrots

Cooking Time: about 2 hours.
Oven: 180°C, 350°F, Gas Mark 4.

To make a crown of lamb, remove the chine bones from the best ends. Cut across the bone ends of the meat about 2·5 cm (1 in) from the bone tips and scrape away all the fat and flesh to leave the bones bare. Place the joints back to back and sew together with the bones curving outwards to give a crown shape, using a trussing needle and fine string. Brush lightly all over with oil.
To make the stuffing, melt the butter in a pan and fry the onion and celery until soft, then stir in all the other ingredients, binding together with the egg. Use to fill the centre of the crown giving a domed top.
Weigh the stuffed crown and place in a roasting tin. Cover the bone tips with foil to prevent burning, and cover the stuffing with foil to keep it moist during cooking. Cook in a moderate oven, allowing 30 minutes per 450 g (1 lb) weight and 30 minutes over. Baste outside of the crown once or twice during cooking and remove the foil from the stuffing for the last half hour.
To serve, place the crown on a serving dish and remove the foil. Decorate bone tips with cutlet frills and surround the crown with whole carrots and peas. Use the pan drippings to make a thin gravy.

Spring lamb cobbler; Crispy lamb; Chilli lamb chops; Armoured cutlets

Armoured cutlets

Metric

225 g frozen puff pastry, thawed
4 lamb cutlets
25 g butter
1 × 5 ml spoon curry powder
Salt and freshly ground black pepper
1 egg, beaten

To garnish:
Lettuce leaves
Mustard and cress

Imperial

8 oz frozen puff pastry, thawed
4 lamb cutlets
1 oz butter
1 teaspoon curry powder
Salt and freshly ground black pepper
1 egg, beaten

To garnish:
Lettuce leaves
Mustard and cress

Cooking Time: 30 minutes.
Oven: 230°C, 450°F, Gas Mark 8.
180°C, 350°F, Gas Mark 4.

On a floured surface roll out the pastry into a narrow strip. Leave to rest.

Trim any excess fat and gristle from the cutlets. Soften the butter and beat in the curry powder and seasonings to taste, then spread evenly over one side of each cutlet. Cut the pastry lengthwise into strips about 2·5 cm (1 in) wide and brush with beaten egg. Use the pastry to wind evenly round the cutlets in overlapping circles until completely enclosed, keeping the egg-glazed side on the outside. Place on a greased baking sheet and cook in a very hot oven for 10 minutes. Reduce oven temperature to moderate and continue for a further 20 minutes or until well browned and puffy.

Serve hot garnished with lettuce and mustard and cress.

Chilli lamb chops

Metric	Imperial
4 loin of lamb chops	4 loin of lamb chops
Salt and freshly ground black pepper	Salt and freshly ground black pepper
4 thin slices of lemon	4 thin slices of lemon
2 large onions, peeled and thinly sliced	2 large onions, peeled and thinly sliced
2 × 5 ml spoons chilli powder	2 teaspoons chilli powder
298 g can condensed tomato soup	10½ oz can condensed tomato soup
To garnish:	To garnish:
Lemon slices	Lemon slices
parsley sprigs	parsley sprigs

Cooking Time: about 45 minutes.
Oven: 200°C, 400°F, Gas Mark 6.

Trim the chops, season lightly and place in a shallow oven-proof dish with a slice of lemon on each one. Blanch the onions in boiling water for 3 minutes then drain thoroughly and lay over the chops. Mix the chilli powder into the soup with seasonings and heat gently. Pour over the chops, cover and cook in a moderately hot oven for about 45 minutes until tender.

Remove any excess fat from the surface, taste and adjust seasonings and garnish with lemon slices and parsley sprigs.

Crispy lamb

Metric	Imperial
1 large or 2 small breasts of lamb, boned	1 large or 2 small breasts of lamb, boned
Salt and freshly ground black pepper	Salt and freshly ground black pepper
1 egg, beaten	1 egg, beaten
Golden crumbs for coating	Golden crumbs for coating
Deep fat for frying	Deep fat for frying
6 × 15 ml spoons thick mayonnaise	6 tablespoons thick mayonnaise
2 × 15 ml spoons capers	2 tablespoons capers
1 × 15 ml spoon finely chopped parsley	1 tablespoon finely chopped parsley
To garnish:	To garnish:
Lemon wedges	Lemon wedges

Cooking Time: about 30 minutes.

Trim the lamb of skin, gristle and excess fat. Place in a saucepan of well seasoned water and bring to the boil. Cover and simmer for 15 minutes then drain the lamb and cool. Cut into narrow strips; dip into the beaten egg and then coat thoroughly in breadcrumbs. Chill until required. Heat the fat to 180°C/350°F, or until a cube of bread browns in it in 30 seconds, and fry the lamb, a few pieces at a time, for 4 to 5 minutes until golden brown. Drain on absorbent paper and keep warm.

Mix together the mayonnaise, capers and parsley, add seasonings to taste and place in a bowl. Serve with the hot crispy lamb garnished with lemon wedges.

Spring lamb cobbler

Metric	Imperial
900 g middle neck of lamb	2 lb middle neck of lamb
25 g dripping or lard	1 oz dripping or lard
2 × 15 ml spoons flour	2 tablespoons flour
2 × 15 ml spoons tomato purée	2 tablespoons tomato purée
600 ml stock or water	1 pint stock or water
4 onions, peeled and sliced	4 onions, peeled and sliced
2 leeks, cleaned and sliced	2 leeks, cleaned and sliced
4 carrots, peeled and sliced	4 carrots, peeled and sliced
1 bay leaf	1 bay leaf
Salt and freshly ground black pepper	Salt and freshly ground black pepper
Scone topping:	Scone topping:
200 g self-raising flour	8 oz self-raising flour
50 g butter or margarine	2 oz butter or margarine
1 egg, beaten	1 egg, beaten
4 × 15 ml spoons milk	4 tablespoons milk

Cooking Time: about 1¾ hours.
Oven: 220°C, 425°F, Gas Mark 7.

Trim the meat and cut into serving pieces. Melt the fat in a flameproof casserole and fry the meat until evenly browned. Dredge with the seasoned flour and continue to cook until flour is browned. Gradually stir in the tomato purée and stock and bring to the boil. Add the onions, leeks, carrots, bay leaf and seasonings and simmer for about 1¼ hours until tender. Discard the bay leaf, taste and adjust seasonings.

Sieve the flour with a pinch of salt into a bowl, add the fat and rub in until the mixture resembles fine breadcrumbs. Add the beaten egg and sufficient milk to mix to a fairly soft dough. Roll out the dough to 1·5 cm (½ in) thickness, cut into 5 cm (2 in) rounds and place in an overlapping circle around the edge of the casserole to make a border on top of the lamb. Brush with milk and cook in a hot oven for 10 to 15 minutes until well risen, golden brown and firm to the touch. Serve at once.

Lamb beanpot

Lamb beanpot

Metric	Imperial
2 breasts of lamb	2 breasts of lamb
1 × 15 ml spoon dripping	1 tablespoon dripping
2 onions, peeled and sliced	2 onions, peeled and sliced
1–2 cloves garlic, crushed	1–2 cloves garlic, crushed
2 large carrots, peeled and sliced	2 large carrots, peeled and sliced
1 × 15 ml spoon flour	1 tablespoon flour
300 ml stock	½ pint stock
4 × 15 ml spoons white wine or cider	4 tablespoons white wine or cider
226 g can peeled tomatoes	8 oz can peeled tomatoes
Salt and freshly ground black pepper	Salt and freshly ground black pepper
425 g can red kidney beans, drained	15 oz can red kidney beans, drained
25 g Edam cheese, grated	1 oz Edam cheese, grated
25 g browned breadcrumbs	1 oz browned breadcrumbs

Cooking Time: about 1½ hours.

Trim the lamb of skin, gristle and fat and cut into thin strips. Fry in the melted dripping until golden brown, then remove from the pan.

Drain off all but 1 × 15 ml spoon (1 tablespoon) fat from the pan then fry the onions, garlic and carrots for 4 to 5 minutes, stirring frequently. Sprinkle in the flour and cook for 1 minute. Gradually add the stock and wine or cider and bring to the boil. Add the tomatoes and seasonings, return the lamb to the pan and cover. Simmer gently for 30 minutes, adding a little more stock, if necessary.

Add the drained beans and continue for about 40 minutes or until tender. Taste and adjust the seasonings and skim off any fat from the surface.

Sprinkle the top with a mixture of the cheese and crumbs and brown under a hot grill.

Lamb noisettes with spicy tomato sauce

Lamb noisettes with spicy tomato sauce

Metric

50 g butter or margarine
4 noisettes of lamb or
loin or chump chops
Salt and freshly ground
black pepper
1–2 cloves garlic,
crushed
100 g button mushrooms,
cleaned, trimmed and
sliced
150 ml red wine
(Burgundy type)
150 ml tomato ketchup
150 ml beef stock
2 × 5 ml spoons cornflour
(optional)

To garnish:
Watercress sprigs
Fried bread triangles

Imperial

2 oz butter or margarine
4 noisettes of lamb or
loin or chump chops
Salt and freshly ground
black pepper
1–2 cloves garlic,
crushed
4 oz button mushrooms,
cleaned, trimmed and
sliced
$\frac{1}{4}$ pint red wine
(Burgundy type)
$\frac{1}{4}$ pint tomato ketchup
$\frac{1}{4}$ pint beef stock
2 teaspoons cornflour
(optional)

To garnish:
Watercress sprigs
Fried bread triangles

Cooking Time: about 30 minutes.

Melt 25 g (1 oz) of the butter in a frying pan. Season the noisettes generously and put into the melted fat. Cover the pan and cook gently for 8 to 10 minutes. Turn the noisettes over and continue for a further 8 to 10 minutes until cooked right through.

Meanwhile melt the remaining butter in a small pan and fry the garlic for 1 to 2 minutes. Add the mushrooms and continue gently for 2 to 3 minutes. Stir in the wine, ketchup and stock, add seasonings and bring to the boil. Simmer gently, uncovered, for 10 to 15 minutes, stirring occasionally, until slightly reduced. Thicken with cornflour blended in a little cold water (if using) and bring back to the boil for 2 minutes. Taste and adjust seasonings.

Drain noisettes on absorbent kitchen paper, then serve with the sauce spooned over, garnished with watercress and fried bread.

Note: cook chops in the same way as noisettes.

29

Boiled lamb with dill sauce

Metric	Imperial
1¼ kg best end of neck of lamb	2½ lb best end of neck of lamb
Salt and freshly ground black pepper	Salt and freshly ground black pepper
1 bay leaf	1 bay leaf
Fresh dill sprigs (see note)	Fresh dill sprigs (see note)
Sauce:	Sauce:
50 g butter	2 oz butter
50 g flour	2 oz flour
2 × 15 ml spoons wine vinegar	2 tablespoons wine vinegar
1 × 15 ml spoon lemon juice	1 tablespoon lemon juice
2 × 5 ml spoons sugar	2 teaspoons sugar
1 egg yolk	1 egg yolk
2 × 15 ml spoons double cream	2 tablespoons double cream
2 × 15 ml spoons finely chopped dill (see note)	2 tablespoons finely chopped dill (see note)

Cooking Time: about 1½ hours.

Trim the lamb and put in a saucepan with the seasonings, bay leaf and sprigs of dill. Add about 1¼ litres (2 pints) water and bring to the boil. Remove any scum from the surface, cover and simmer gently for 1¼–1½ hours or until tender. Drain the joint and keep warm.

Strain and reserve 600 ml (1 pint) cooking liquor. Melt the butter in a pan, stir in the flour and cook for 1 minute. Gradually add the liquor and bring to the boil for 2 minutes, stirring continuously. Remove from the heat. Add the vinegar, lemon juice, sugar, egg yolk, cream and half the dill and reheat gently without boiling. Taste and adjust the seasonings.

Serve the lamb with some sauce poured over and with the remaining dill sprinkled on top. Garnish with parsley sprigs, if liked.

Note: dried dill can be used when fresh dill is not available; or drained capers can be used instead.

Stuffed onion dumplings

Metric	Imperial
4 medium-sized onions (175–225 g each), peeled	4 medium-sized onions (6–8 oz each), peeled
Salt and freshly ground black pepper	Salt and freshly ground black pepper
Filling:	Filling:
25 g butter	1 oz butter
50 g mushrooms, cleaned trimmed and chopped	2 oz mushrooms, cleaned, trimmed and chopped
1 clove garlic, crushed	1 clove garlic, crushed
4 rashers streaky bacon, derinded and chopped	4 rashers streaky bacon, derinded and chopped
225 g cooked lamb, finely chopped or minced	8 oz cooked lamb, finely chopped or minced
8 stuffed olives, chopped	8 stuffed olives, chopped
50 g cooked rice	2 oz cooked rice
Pastry:	Pastry:
300 g plain flour	12 oz plain flour
Pinch of salt	Pinch of salt
75 g margarine	3 oz margarine
75 g lard or white fat	3 oz lard or white fat
Water to mix	Water to mix
Beaten egg or milk to glaze	Beaten egg or milk to glaze

Cooking Time: about 1¾ hours.
Oven: 200°C, 400°F, Gas Mark 6.
160°C, 325°F, Gas Mark 3.

Cook the onions in boiling salted water for 10 minutes then drain and leave to cool.

Melt the butter and fry the mushrooms, garlic and bacon gently for 5 minutes. Stir in the lamb, olives, rice and season well, cool.

Sieve the flour with a pinch of salt into a bowl, add the fats rub in until the mixture resembles fine breadcrumbs. Add sufficient water to mix to a pliable dough.

Using a small spoon, scoop out the centres of the onions leaving an outer shell and base about 1 cm (½ in) thick. Fill the centre with the lamb mixture pressing it well in. Roll out the pastry and cut into 4 rounds about 20 cm (8 in) in diameter. Place the onions, filling end downwards, on the pastry, dampen pastry edges and wrap round to completely enclose the onions in pastry.

Stand the dumplings in a lightly greased baking tin with the seams underneath. Decorate the tops with pastry leaves made from the trimmings and brush with egg or milk. Cook in moderately hot oven for 20 minutes then reduce oven temperature to warm and continue for a further 1–1¼ hours, until the onions feel tender when pierced with a skewer. Serve hot.

Note: use the scooped-out insides of the onions in some other dish or soup.

Stuffed onion dumplings; Boiled lamb with dill sauce; Chinese cutlets

Chinese cutlets

Metric

4 lamb cutlets
Salt and freshly ground
black pepper
300 ml chicken stock
2 × 15 ml spoons tomato
ketchup
1 × 15 ml spoon soy sauce
2 × 5 ml spoons cornflour
1 onion, peeled and
chopped
1 green pepper, washed,
deseeded and sliced
1 × 15 ml spoon oil
175 g mushrooms, cleaned
trimmed and sliced
454 g can bean sprouts,
drained
1 × 15 ml spoon sherry
2 eggs
25 g butter

Imperial

4 lamb cutlets
Salt and freshly ground
black pepper
½ pint chicken stock
2 tablespoons tomato
ketchup
1 tablespoon soy sauce
2 teaspoons cornflour
1 onion, peeled and
chopped
1 green pepper, washed,
deseeded and sliced
1 tablespoon oil
6 oz mushrooms, cleaned,
trimmed and sliced
16 oz can bean sprouts,
drained
1 tablespoon sherry
2 eggs
1 oz butter

Cooking Time: about 30 minutes.

Trim the cutlets, season well and cook on the grill rack under a moderate heat for 8 to 10 minutes each side.

Meanwhile, to make the sauce, place the stock, ketchup and soy sauce in a pan, add seasonings, blend in the cornflour and bring to the boil, stirring continuously, for 3 minutes.

Fry the onion and pepper in oil until soft, add the mushrooms and continue for 5 minutes. Stir in the bean sprouts, sherry and one-third of the sauce and simmer for 5 minutes.

Beat the eggs with seasonings and 2 × 15 ml spoons (2 tablespoons) water and use, with the butter, to make two large flat omelettes in a frying pan. Cut each in half.

To serve, place the bean sprout mixture in a hot serving dish. Place the cutlets on top. Roll up each piece of omelette and lay on the cutlets. Serve the remaining sauce in a sauce boat.

Pot roast lamb with fennel; Lamb cutlets Arlene; Lancashire-style hotpot; Minted lamb pasties

Lancashire-style hotpot

Metric

8 middle neck lamb chops
2 lambs' kidneys, skinned,
cored and roughly
chopped
2 onions, peeled and
sliced
2 carrots, peeled and
diced
1 small turnip, peeled
and diced
Salt and freshly ground
black pepper
300 ml stock
450 g potatoes, peeled
and thinly sliced

Imperial

8 middle neck lamb chops
2 lambs' kidneys, skinned,
cored and roughly
chopped
2 onions, peeled and
sliced
2 carrots, peeled and
diced
1 small turnip, peeled
and diced
Salt and freshly ground
black pepper
½ pint stock
1 lb potatoes, peeled
and thinly sliced

Cooking Time: about 2½ hours.
Oven: 160°C, 325°F, Gas Mark 3.
       200°C, 400°F, Gas Mark 6.

Trim the chops, removing any excess fat, and place in an ovenproof casserole. Add the kidneys, onions, carrots, turnip and plenty of seasonings. Pour in the stock and arrange the potatoes in overlapping circles over the contents of the casserole. Cover and cook in warm oven for about 2 hours or until the meat and potatoes are tender. Remove the lid, raise oven temperature to moderately hot and continue for about 20 minutes to brown the potatoes.
Note: two or three sprigs of fresh mint can be added to this casserole when available.

Lamb cutlets Arlene

Metric	Imperial
8 lamb cutlets	8 lamb cutlets
Salt and black pepper	Salt and black pepper
40 g butter	1½ oz butter
175 g mushrooms, cleaned trimmed and chopped	6 oz mushrooms, cleaned, trimmed and chopped
3 × 15 ml spoons capers	3 tablespoons capers
6 × 15 ml spoons chopped gherkins	6 tablespoons chopped gherkins
1 × 15 ml spoon wine vinegar	1 tablespoon wine vinegar

Cooking Time: about 25 minutes.

Trim cutlets and season well. Place on a grill rack and dot with 15 g (½ oz) butter. Cook under a moderate grill for 8 to 10 minutes each side until just cooked through.

Meanwhile, melt the remaining butter in a pan and fry the mushrooms until soft. Add the capers, gherkins, vinegar and seasonings and cook gently for 5 minutes.

Serve the lamb cutlets on a hot dish, decorated with cutlet frills, if liked, and the mushroom mixture spooned over the eyes of the cutlets. Garnish with parsley, tomato wedges, if liked.

Pot roast lamb with fennel

Metric	Imperial
1½ kg loin of lamb joint	3 lb loin of lamb joint
1 × 15 ml spoon dripping	1 tablespoon dripping
Salt and freshly ground black pepper	Salt and freshly ground black pepper
1 large bulb of fennel, cleaned and roughly chopped	1 large bulb of fennel, cleaned and roughly chopped
1 onion, peeled and chopped	1 onion, peeled and chopped
½ teaspoon finely grated lemon rind	½ teaspoon finely grated lemon rind
1 × 15 ml spoon lemon juice	1 tablespoon lemon juice
About 300 ml boiling stock	About ½ pint boiling stock
1 × 15 ml spoon cornflour	1 tablespoon cornflour

Cooking Time: about 1½ hours.
Oven: 190°C, 375°F, Gas Mark 5.

Trim the lamb and brown the joint all over in melted dripping. Place in an ovenproof casserole and season well. Arrange the fennel and onion around the joint, add the lemon rind and juice and stock. Cover tightly and cook in a moderately hot oven for about 1½ hours or until tender.

Strain off the cooking liquor, make up to 300 ml (½ pint) with more stock if necessary and thicken with the cornflour blended in a little cold water. Boil for 2 minutes, taste and adjust the seasonings.

Slice the lamb, surround it with the fennel and serve with the sauce.

Serves 6.

Minted lamb pasties

Metric	Imperial
200 g plain flour	8 oz plain flour
Pinch of salt	Pinch of salt
50 g margarine	2 oz margarine
50 g lard or white fat	2 oz lard or white fat
Water to mix	Water to mix
175 g cooked lamb, finely diced	6 oz cooked lamb, finely diced
1 small onion, peeled and finely chopped	1 small onion, peeled and finely chopped
3 × 15 ml spoons cooked peas	3 tablespoons cooked peas
100 g boiled potatoes, chopped	4 oz boiled potatoes, chopped
Salt and freshly ground black pepper	Salt and freshly ground black pepper
2 × 5 ml spoons freshly chopped mint or 1 × 5 ml spoon dried mint	2 teaspoons freshly chopped mint or 1 teaspoon dried mint
Beaten egg to glaze	Beaten egg to glaze

Cooking Time: 30–35 minutes.
Oven: 220°C, 425°F, Gas Mark 7.
 180°C, 350°F, Gas Mark 4.

Sieve the flour with a pinch of salt into a bowl. Add the fats and rub in until the mixture resembles fine breadcrumbs. Add sufficient cold water to mix to a pliable dough and knead lightly until smooth. Wrap in foil and chill for 30 minutes if possible.

Mix together the chopped lamb, onion, peas, potato, salt and pepper to taste and the mint.

Roll out the pastry on a floured surface and cut into four circles 18 cm (7 in) in diameter. Divide the meat mixture between these, placing it in the centre of each. Damp the pastry edges and bring together at the top to form a pasty. Press well together and crimp the edge. Place on a dampened baking sheet and brush with beaten egg. Cook in a hot oven for 15 minutes, then reduce oven temperature to moderate and continue for 15 to 20 minutes, until well browned.

Serve hot or cold with tomato wedges.

Note: if using raw diced lamb, fry gently in 25 g (1 oz) butter for 5 to 10 minutes before mixing with the other ingredients.

33

Roast apricot lamb

Roast apricot lamb

Metric

100 g dried apricots,
soaked overnight
25 g butter
1 medium-sized onion,
peeled and finely chopped
Finely grated rind of ½
lemon
2 × 15 ml spoons finely
chopped parsley
Salt and freshly ground
black pepper
Good pinch of ground
mixed spice
50 g long-grain rice,
cooked
1 small egg, beaten
Small shoulder of lamb,
boned (about 1½ kg)
A little dripping or oil
300 ml stock
2–3 × 5 ml spoons
cornflour

Imperial

4 oz dried apricots,
soaked overnight
1 oz butter
1 medium-sized onion,
peeled and finely chopped
Finely grated rind of ½
lemon
2 tablespoons finely
chopped parsley
Salt and freshly ground
black pepper
Good pinch of ground
mixed spice
2 oz long-grain rice,
cooked
1 small egg, beaten
Small shoulder of lamb,
boned (about 3 lb)
A little dripping or oil
½ pint stock
2–3 teaspoons cornflour

Cooking Time: about 2 hours.
Oven: 220°C, 425°F, Gas Mark 7.

To make the stuffing, cook the apricots in the soaking water for 10 minutes then drain, reserving the liquor; chop the fruit. Melt the butter and fry the onion gently until soft. Remove from the heat and stir in the lemon rind, parsley, seasonings, spice, cooked rice and apricots; bind together with the egg.

Put the lamb on to a board and spread the stuffing over the inside. Roll the joint carefully making sure all the stuffing is enclosed. Secure with skewers and string and weigh the joint. Place in a roasting tin, spread with a little dripping and season lightly. Cook in a hot oven, allowing 25 minutes per 450 g (1 lb) weight and 25 minutes over, basting occasionally. Remove the joint and keep warm. Use the pan drippings, 150 ml (¼ pint) reserved apricot juice, stock and seasonings to taste to make a gravy, and thicken with the cornflour blended in a little cold water.
Serves 6.

Fillet of lamb en croûte

Fillet of lamb en croûte

Metric	Imperial
2 large fillets of lamb	2 large fillets of lamb
25 g butter	1 oz butter
1 small onion, peeled and finely chopped	1 small onion, peeled and finely chopped
1 clove garlic, crushed	1 clove garlic, crushed
100 g mushrooms, cleaned, trimmed and chopped	4 oz mushrooms, cleaned, trimmed and chopped
Salt and freshly ground black pepper	Salt and freshly ground black pepper
1 × 5 ml spoon dried rosemary	1 teaspoon dried rosemary
1 × 15 ml spoon finely chopped parsley	1 tablespoon finely chopped parsley
350 g frozen puff pastry, thawed	12 oz frozen puff pastry, thawed
Beaten egg to glaze	Beaten egg to glaze

To garnish:
Rosemary sprigs
(if available)
Potato croquettes

To garnish:
Rosemary sprigs
(if available)
Potato croquettes

Cooking Time: 1–1¼ hours.
Oven: 230°C, 450°F, Gas Mark 8.
190°C, 375°F, Gas Mark 5.

Trim the lamb fillets and lay one on top of the other. Secure with thin string. Fry quickly in hot melted butter until sealed all over. Remove and cool.

Fry the onion and garlic in the same fat until soft, then stir in the mushrooms and cook gently for 3 to 4 minutes. Remove from the heat, season well and stir in the rosemary and parsley and leave to cool.

Roll out the pastry to a rectangle. Spread the mushroom mixture in a strip down the centre of the pastry. Remove the string from the lamb and lay lamb on top of the mush-rooms. Fold over the pastry to enclose the lamb, dampening the edges to seal. Place on a dampened baking sheet with the joins underneath and decorate the top with pastry trimmings. Brush with beaten egg and cook in a very hot oven for 10 minutes, then reduce oven temperature to moderately hot and continue for 50 to 60 minutes until the pastry is golden brown. Cover the pastry with foil when sufficiently browned.

Serve in slices, garnished with sprigs of fresh rosemary, and potato croquettes, with a thin gravy.

Honeyed lamb chops; Curried neck of lamb; Stuffed breasts of lamb; Spanish lamb chops

Stuffed breasts of lamb

Metric

2 large breasts of lamb, boned
Salt and freshly ground black pepper
65 g butter
2 medium-sized onions, peeled and chopped
75 g cooked rice
50 g raisins
2 × 5 ml spoons dried thyme
40 g flour
300 ml stock
150 ml dry cider or white wine

To garnish:
Fresh thyme or parsley

36

Imperial

2 large breasts of lamb, boned
Salt and freshly ground black pepper
2½ oz butter
2 medium-sized onions, peeled and chopped
3 oz cooked rice
2 oz raisins
2 teaspoons dried thyme
1½ oz flour
½ pint stock
¼ pint dry cider or white wine

To garnish:
Fresh thyme or parsley

Cooking Time: 50 minutes–1 hour.
Oven: 220°C, 425°F, Gas Mark 7.

Trim the breasts of lamb of any gristle, membrane and excess fat. Cut each one in half and season lightly. Melt 25 g (1 oz) butter and fry one onion until lightly browned. Stir in the rice, raisins, half the thyme and plenty of seasonings. Divide stuffing between the four pieces of lamb, spreading it evenly over the inside of the meat. Roll each piece up and secure with wooden cocktail sticks. Place in a roasting tin and cook in a hot oven for ¾ to 1 hour, or until well browned and cooked through. Baste several times during cooking. Remove to a serving dish and keep warm. To make the sauce, melt the remaining butter and fry the second onion until soft. Stir in the flour and cook for 1 minute, then gradually add the stock and cider or wine and bring to the boil for 2 minutes. Add the remaining thyme and seasonings to taste. Garnish the lamb with fresh herbs, and serve with the sauce.

Honeyed lamb chops

Metric	Imperial
4 loin of lamb chops	4 loin of lamb chops
Salt and freshly ground black pepper	Salt and freshly ground black pepper
15 g butter	½ oz butter
1 × 15 ml spoon finely chopped mint	1 tablespoon finely chopped mint
2–3 × 15 ml spoons honey	2–3 tablespoons honey
½ teaspoon finely grated lemon rind	½ teaspoon finely grated lemon rind
To garnish:	To garnish:
Lemon slices	Lemon slices

Cooking Time: about 20 minutes.

Trim the lamb and season lightly. Place in a grill pan and dot with butter. Cook under a moderate grill for 8 to 10 minutes until well browned. Turn the chops over and continue for 2 to 3 minutes.

Mix together the mint, honey and lemon rind and spread over the chops. Continue to cook for 5 to 8 minutes until well browned and cooked through. Serve with the pan juices spooned over, and garnish with lemon slices, and sprigs of fresh mint, when available.

Curried neck of lamb

Metric	Imperial
1¼ kg middle neck of lamb	2½ lb middle neck of lamb
1 × 15 ml spoon ground coriander	1 tablespoon ground coriander
1 × 5 ml spoon turmeric	1 teaspoon turmeric
½ teaspoon powdered cummin	½ teaspoon powdered cummin
¼ teaspoon chilli powder	¼ teaspoon chilli powder
¼ teaspoon ground cinnamon	¼ teaspoon ground cinnamon
Pinch of ground cloves	Pinch of ground cloves
1–2 × 5 ml spoons curry paste	1–2 teaspoons curry paste
25 g dripping or lard	1 oz dripping or lard
2 onions, peeled and sliced	2 onions, peeled and sliced
1 clove garlic, crushed	1 clove garlic, crushed
450 ml stock or water	¾ pint stock or water
Salt and freshly ground black pepper	Salt and freshly ground black pepper

Cooking Time: about 2 hours.

Trim the lamb and cut into small pieces. Combine the spices with the curry paste and a little water to mix. Melt the fat in a pan and fry the onions and garlic until soft. Add the spice paste and fry for 5 minutes, stirring frequently. Add the meat, mixing well, and cook gently for about 15 minutes, turning occasionally. Add the stock and bring to the boil. Cover and simmer gently for about 1½ hours or until tender. Add a little more boiling liquid if necessary during cooking, but there should not be too much liquid at the end, as this is a dryish type of curry.

Taste and adjust seasonings and serve with freshly boiled rice and a selection of curry accompaniments: ie, poppadums, mango chutney, salted peanuts, sliced tomatoes with onion, sliced banana, etc.

Note: whole coriander can be used if you crush the seeds thoroughly first.

Spanish lamb chops

Metric	Imperial
25 g butter	1 oz butter
4 loin of lamb chops	4 loin of lamb chops
1 large onion, peeled and sliced	1 large onion, peeled and sliced
1 clove garlic, crushed	1 clove garlic, crushed
1 pepper (red or green), deseeded and chopped	1 pepper (red or green), deseeded and chopped
175 g long-grain rice	6 oz long-grain rice
About 750 ml stock	About 1¼ pints stock
Pinch of saffron or ½ teaspoon turmeric	Pinch of saffron or ½ teaspoon turmeric
Salt and freshly ground black pepper	Salt and freshly ground black pepper
100 g frozen peas	4 oz frozen peas

Cooking Time: 50–55 minutes.

Melt the butter in a large heavy frying pan and brown the chops on both sides. Remove from the pan. Fry the onion, garlic and pepper in the same fat until soft. Stir in the rice and continue for 2 minutes. Add the stock, saffron or turmeric and seasonings and bring to the boil. Replace the chops and cover the pan. Simmer gently for 20 minutes. Turn the chops over, stir in the peas and add a little more boiling stock if necessary. Re-cover and continue to simmer gently for about 20 minutes or until the lamb and rice are tender and the liquid has been absorbed. Taste and adjust the seasonings and serve straight from the pan.

Note: a few mussels and/or peeled prawns can be added to the rice, if liked, with the peas.

Aubergine moussaka

Metric	Imperial
675 g aubergines (about 3)	1½ lb aubergines (about 3)
Salt and freshly ground black pepper	Salt and freshly ground black pepper
3–4 × 15 ml spoons oil	3–4 tablespoons oil
2 large onions, peeled and thinly sliced	2 large onions, peeled and thinly sliced
450 g lean raw lamb, minced	1 lb lean raw lamb, minced
226 g can peeled tomatoes	8 oz can peeled tomatoes
2 × 15 ml spoons tomato purée	2 tablespoons tomato purée
4 × 15 ml spoons stock	4 tablespoons stock
Topping:	Topping:
2 large eggs	2 large eggs
100 g plain cottage cheese, sieved	4 oz plain cottage cheese, sieved
6 × 15 ml spoons single cream	6 tablespoons single cream

Cooking Time: about 1½ hours.
Oven: 180°C, 350°F, Gas Mark 4.

Wash and dry the aubergines, slice them and sprinkle lightly with salt; leave to stand for 30 minutes. Rinse off the salt, drain thoroughly and dry on absorbent kitchen paper. Fry the aubergines in 2–3 × 15 ml spoons (2–3 tablespoons) oil until lightly browned. Drain and use to line a large shallow ovenproof casserole.

Fry the onions in the remaining oil until soft then add the meat and cook gently for about 10 minutes, stirring occasionally. Add the tomatoes, tomato purée, stock and plenty of seasonings and cook for a further 5 minutes. Spoon over the aubergines and cook, uncovered, in a moderate oven for about 45 minutes, until cooked through.

Beat together the eggs, cottage cheese and cream, season well and spoon over the meat. Return to the oven for a further 25 to 30 minutes until the topping is set and lightly browned.

Note: raw minced beef may be used in place of lamb.

Aubergine moussaka

Roast pork with bacon and sage

Metric

1¼ kg loin of pork, boned and rolled
Salt and freshly ground black pepper
6 rashers lean back bacon, derinded
2 × 5 ml spoons freshly chopped sage, or 1 × 5 ml spoon dried sage
40 g fresh breadcrumbs
1 egg yolk
A little oil
2 × 5 ml spoons flour
300 ml stock
1 × 5 ml spoon tomato purée

Imperial

2½ lb loin of pork, boned and rolled
Salt and freshly ground black pepper
6 rashers lean back bacon, derinded
2 teaspoons freshly chopped sage, or 1 teaspoon dried sage
1½ oz fresh breadcrumbs
1 egg yolk
A little oil
2 teaspoons flour
½ pint stock
1 teaspoon tomato purée

Cooking Time: about 1¾–2 hours.
Oven: 190°C, 375°F, Gas Mark 5.

Unroll the pork and cut the flesh a little to open it out. Season the inside lightly and lay the bacon evenly over the surface. Combine the sage and breadcrumbs and bind together with the egg yolk. Spread over the bacon. Re-roll the pork to enclose the filling. Secure with string and skewers and weigh the joint. Place in a roasting tin, rub the rind with oil and then with salt. Cook in a moderately hot oven, allowing 30–35 minutes per 450 g (1 lb) weight, plus 30 minutes over (depending on the thickness of the joint). Baste occasionally. Remove the joint to a serving dish and keep warm.

Drain off the fat from the pan but reserve 1 × 15 ml spoon (1 tablespoon). Stir the flour into this fat and cook for a few minutes until beginning to brown. Stir in the stock and tomato purée, season and bring to the boil for 3 minutes. Serve the gravy with the sliced joint.

Serves 6.

Roast pork with bacon and sage

Stroganoff-style pork; Cheesy topped pork; Barbecued pork; Pork stuffed peppers

Barbecued pork

Metric

25 g butter
1 × 5 ml spoon oil
900 g pork spare ribs
(American-style)
2 large onions, peeled
and sliced
4 × 15 ml spoons
demerara sugar
1½ × 5 ml spoons salt
1 × 5 ml spoon paprika
1 × 15 ml spoon tomato
purée
1 × 15 ml spoon
Worcestershire sauce
2 × 15 ml spoons malt
vinegar
4 × 15 ml spoons lemon
juice
200 ml water
175 g dried apricots,
soaked overnight, or a
425 g can apricots,
halved and drained

To garnish:
Black olives

Imperial

1 oz butter
1 teaspoon oil
2 lb pork spare ribs
(American-style)
2 large onions, peeled
and sliced
4 tablespoons demerara
sugar
1½ teaspoons salt
1 teaspoon paprika
1 tablespoon tomato
purée
1 tablespoon
Worcestershire sauce
2 tablespoons malt
vinegar
4 tablespoons lemon juice
7 fl oz water
6 oz dried apricots,
soaked overnight, or a
15 oz can apricots,
halved and drained

To garnish:
Black olives

Cooking Time: 1¼–1½ hours.
Oven: 200°C, 400°F, Gas Mark 6.

Melt the butter in a pan, add the oil and then fry the spare ribs quickly until browned. Transfer to an ovenproof casserole.

Fry the onions in the same fat until lightly browned, then drain off any excess fat from the pan. Blend together all the other ingredients, except the apricots, and add to the onion. Bring to the boil and simmer for 3 to 4 minutes. Pour over the pork, cover and cook in a moderately hot oven for 45 minutes, basting several times.

Drain the apricots and add to the sauce. Return to the oven for a further 15 to 30 minutes, until really tender. Spoon off any excess fat from the surface and serve garnished with olives.

Cheesy topped pork

Metric	Imperial
4 lean pork chops	4 lean pork chops
Salt and freshly ground black pepper	Salt and freshly ground black pepper
25 g butter	1 oz butter
1 green pepper, washed, deseeded and thinly sliced	1 green pepper, washed, deseeded and thinly sliced
4 tomatoes, peeled and sliced	4 tomatoes, peeled and sliced
1½ × 5 ml spoons dried rosemary	1½ teaspoons dried rosemary
50 g Cheddar cheese, grated	2 oz Cheddar cheese, grated

Cooking Time: 25 to 30 minutes.

Trim the pork and season lightly on both sides. Cook in the grill pan under a moderate heat for about 10 minutes. Meanwhile melt the butter in a small pan and fry the pepper until soft. Turn the chops over and cook for a further 8 to 10 minutes until cooked through. Spoon the peppers on top of the chops, cover with sliced tomatoes and sprinkle with the herbs. Place under the grill for 3 to 4 minutes to heat through the topping. Sprinkle with cheese and return to a hot grill until brown and bubbling. Serve at once.

Pork stuffed peppers

Metric	Imperial
65 g butter	2½ oz butter
1 onion, peeled and finely chopped	1 onion, peeled and finely chopped
4 rashers streaky bacon, derinded and chopped	4 rashers streaky bacon, derinded and chopped
450 g lean minced pork	1 lb lean minced pork
25 g fresh breadcrumbs	1 oz fresh breadcrumbs
1–2 × 5 ml spoons dried tarragon	1–2 teaspoons dried tarragon
2 tomatoes, peeled and chopped	2 tomatoes, peeled and chopped
Salt and freshly ground black pepper	Salt and freshly ground black pepper
4 green peppers	4 green peppers
450 ml hot chicken stock	¾ pint hot chicken stock
40 g flour	1½ oz flour

Cooking Time: 1¼ hours.
Oven: 180°C, 350°F, Gas Mark 4.

Melt 25 g (1 oz) butter in a pan and fry the onion and bacon until soft. Add the mince and cook gently for 5 to 10 minutes, stirring frequently. Stir in the breadcrumbs, tarragon, tomatoes and seasonings. Wash and dry the peppers, cut the tops off and remove the seeds. Stand in a greased ovenproof casserole and fill with the pork mixture. Pour the hot stock around the peppers, cover and cook in a moderate oven for ¾–1 hour until tender.
Drain off the cooking liquor and make up to 450 ml (¾ pint) with more stock, if necessary. Keep the peppers warm. Melt the remaining butter in a pan, stir in the flour and cook for 1 minute. Gradually add the cooking liquor and bring to the boil for 3 minutes. Taste and adjust the seasonings. Serve the peppers with the sauce in a sauce boat.

Stroganoff-style pork

Metric	Imperial
550 g pork fillet	1¼ lb pork fillet
25 g butter	1 oz butter
2 × 15 ml spoons oil	2 tablespoons oil
1 onion, peeled and finely sliced	1 onion, peeled and finely sliced
100 g mushrooms, cleaned, trimmed and finely sliced	4 oz mushrooms, cleaned, trimmed and finely sliced
4 tomatoes, peeled and sliced	4 tomatoes, peeled and sliced
200 ml chicken stock	7 fl oz chicken stock
Salt and freshly ground black pepper	Salt and freshly ground black pepper
150 ml soured cream	¼ pint soured cream
To garnish:	To garnish:
Finely chopped parsley	Finely chopped parsley

Cooking Time: about 30 minutes.

Cut the pork into thin strips and fry in a mixture of butter and oil for 5 minutes, stirring occasionally, then remove from the pan. Fry the onion in the same fat until lightly browned, then add the mushrooms and continue for 5 minutes. Add the tomatoes, stock and seasonings and bring to the boil. Return the pork to the pan, cover and simmer for about 20 minutes or until the meat is tender and the liquid is reduced by about half. Stir in the cream and bring back just to the boil. Taste and adjust the seasonings. Serve liberally sprinkled with parsley.

Serendipity chops

Metric	Imperial
4 pork chops	4 pork chops
Salt and freshly ground black pepper	Salt and freshly ground black pepper
25 g butter	1 oz butter
40 g fresh breadcrumbs	1½ oz fresh breadcrumbs
½ teaspoon ground mace	½ teaspoon ground mace
½ teaspoon dried thyme	½ teaspoon dried thyme
1 × 15 ml spoon finely chopped parsley	1 tablespoon finely chopped parsley
25 g shelled walnuts, chopped (optional)	1 oz shelled walnuts, chopped (optional)
4 × 15 ml spoons stock	4 tablespoons stock
To garnish:	To garnish:
Lemon wedges	Lemon wedges
Parsley sprigs	Parsley sprigs

Cooking Time: about 45 minutes.
Oven: 200°C, 400°F, Gas Mark 6.

Trim the chops and season with salt and pepper. Melt the butter in a frying pan and fry the chops quickly on both sides until browned. Transfer to a shallow ovenproof casserole large enough to take the chops in one layer. Mix together the breadcrumbs, mace, thyme, parsley, walnuts (if using) and seasonings to taste. Spoon evenly over the chops and pour the remaining fat in the frying pan over the topping. Add the stock to the casserole and cover with foil or a lid. Cook towards the top of a moderately hot oven for 20 minutes, remove the foil and continue for a further 10 to 20 minutes, until the chops are tender and the topping is crispy. Garnish with lemon wedges and parsley.

Serendipity chops; Boston baked beans

Somerset pork

Somerset pork

Metric	Imperial
4 boneless pork slices	4 boneless pork slices
2 × 15 ml spoons seasoned flour	2 tablespoons seasoned flour
40 g butter	1½ oz butter
175 g button mushrooms, cleaned and trimmed	6 oz button mushrooms, cleaned and trimmed
300 ml dry cider	½ pint dry cider
Good dash of Worcestershire sauce	Good dash of Worcestershire sauce
Salt and freshly ground black pepper	Salt and freshly ground black pepper
100 ml double cream	4 fl oz double cream
Finely chopped parsley, or sprigs	Finely chopped parsley, or sprigs

Cooking Time: about 30 minutes.

Trim the pork and coat in seasoned flour. Fry in the melted butter until browned on both sides and almost cooked through. Remove from the pan and keep warm.
Add the mushrooms to the pan and cook gently for 2 to 3 minutes. Stir in the remaining flour and cook for 1 minute, then gradually add the cider and bring to the boil. Add the Worcestershire sauce and seasonings and replace the pork. Cover and simmer for about 10 minutes. Stir in the cream, taste and adjust the seasonings and reheat without boiling. Serve sprinkled with parsley, or garnished with sprigs.

Boston baked beans

Metric	Imperial
225 g butter beans	8 oz butter beans
450 g belly pork, skinned	1 lb belly pork, skinned
2 large onions, peeled and sliced	2 large onions, peeled and sliced
2 × 5 ml spoons salt	2 teaspoons salt
1½ × 5 ml spoons dry mustard	1½ teaspoons dry mustard
Freshly ground black pepper	Freshly ground black pepper
2 × 15 ml spoons black treacle	2 tablespoons black treacle
2 × 15 ml spoons cider vinegar	2 tablespoons cider vinegar
6 cloves	6 cloves
1 × 5 ml spoon tomato purée	1 teaspoon tomato purée

Cooking Time: 7 hours.
Oven: 150°C, 300°F, Gas Mark 2.

Wash the beans thoroughly and soak in cold water over-night. Drain the beans, reserving the liquor, and place in a large, heavy ovenproof casserole. Trim the pork of any bones and gristle and cut into 2·5 cm (1 in) cubes. Add to the beans with the onion and just enough of the soaking liquor to cover barely. Stir in the remaining ingredients and cover the casserole tightly. Cook in a cool oven for 6 hours. Remove and stir well. Add a little boiling water if getting too dry and taste and adjust the seasonings. Cover and return to the oven for a further hour.

Sweet 'n' sour pork balls

Metric	Imperial
450 g lean pork, minced	1 lb lean pork, minced
1 clove garlic, crushed	1 clove garlic, crushed
50 g fresh breadcrumbs	2 oz fresh breadcrumbs
Salt and freshly ground black pepper	Salt and freshly ground black pepper
1 egg, beaten	1 egg, beaten
Flour for coating	Flour for coating
25 g lard or white fat	1 oz lard or white fat
Sauce:	Sauce:
1 green pepper, washed, deseeded and thinly sliced	1 green pepper, washed, deseeded and thinly sliced
1 red pepper, washed, deseeded and thinly sliced	1 red pepper, washed, deseeded and thinly sliced
Small can crushed pineapple, or 4 canned pineapple rings, chopped	Small can crushed pineapple, or 4 canned pineapple rings, chopped
75 g sugar	3 oz sugar
4 × 15 ml spoons cider vinegar	4 tablespoons cider vinegar
2–3 × 15 ml spoons soy sauce	2–3 tablespoons soy sauce
300 ml stock or water	½ pint stock or water
4 × 5 ml spoons cornflour	4 teaspoons cornflour

Cooking Time: about 45 minutes.

Combine the pork with the garlic, breadcrumbs and plenty of seasonings and bind together with the egg. Divide into 20 pieces and shape into small balls. Dip each in the flour. Heat the lard in a pan and fry the balls gently for 15 to 20 minutes, turning frequently, until golden brown and cooked through, keep warm.

Meanwhile, blanch the peppers for 5 minutes and drain. Mix with the pineapple. Place the sugar in a pan with the vinegar, soy sauce and stock and bring to the boil. Add the peppers and pineapple and simmer for 5 minutes. Blend the cornflour with a little cold water and add to the sauce. Bring back to the boil and simmer for a further 3 to 4 minutes. Taste and adjust the seasonings.

Drain the pork balls on absorbent kitchen paper and serve hot with boiled rice and the sauce spooned over.

Pork goulash

Metric	Imperial
675 g pork fillet	1½ lb pork fillet
50 g butter	2 oz butter
1 × 15 ml spoon oil	1 tablespoon oil
2 onions, peeled and sliced	2 onions, peeled and sliced
1 × 15 ml spoon paprika	1 tablespoon paprika
2 × 15 ml spoons flour	2 tablespoons flour
2 × 5 ml spoons tomato purée	2 teaspoons tomato purée
226 g can peeled tomatoes	8 oz can peeled tomatoes
450 ml stock	¾ pint stock
Salt and freshly ground black pepper	Salt and freshly ground black pepper
1 green pepper, washed, deseeded and thinly sliced	1 green pepper, washed, deseeded and thinly sliced
4 × 15 ml spoons double cream	4 tablespoons double cream
½ teaspoon finely grated lemon rind	½ teaspoon finely grated lemon rind

Cooking Time: about 55 minutes.

Cut the pork into thin strips. Melt 25 g (1 oz) butter and the oil in a pan and fry the pork for 5 minutes. Remove the pork, add the remaining butter to the pan and, when melted, fry the onions until soft. Stir in the paprika, flour and tomato purée and cook for 1 minute. Add the tomatoes and stock, season well and bring to the boil. Add the pepper and return the pork to the pan. Cover and simmer for about 45 minutes until tender.

Taste and adjust the seasonings, mix the cream with the lemon rind, and serve spooned on top of the goulash.

Sweet sour pork balls; Indonesian pork; Pork goulash

Indonesian pork

Metric	Imperial
225 g long-grain rice	8 oz long-grain rice
Salt and freshly ground black pepper	Salt and freshly ground black pepper
65 g butter	2½ oz butter
1 large onion, peeled and chopped	1 large onion, peeled and chopped
2 carrots, peeled and diced	2 carrots, peeled and diced
1 clove garlic, crushed	1 clove garlic, crushed
1½ × 5 ml spoons curry powder	1½ teaspoons curry powder
½ teaspoon ground coriander	½ teaspoon ground coriander
½ teaspoon chilli powder	½ teaspoon chilli powder
½ teaspoon caraway seeds (optional)	½ teaspoon caraway seeds (optional)
1 × 15 ml spoon soy sauce	1 tablespoon soy sauce
350–450 g cold lean roast pork, diced	¾–1 lb cold lean roast pork, diced
225 g frozen peas, freshly cooked	8 oz frozen peas, freshly cooked
1 large egg	1 large egg

Cooking Time: about 40 minutes.

Cook the rice in plenty of boiling salted water until just tender – about 12 minutes. Drain very thoroughly.

Melt 50 g (2 oz) butter in a heavy-based saucepan and fry the onion, carrots and garlic very gently until soft but only lightly coloured, stirring frequently. Add the curry powder, coriander, chilli powder, caraway seeds, soy sauce and seasonings and cook gently for 1 minute. Add the diced pork and continue gently, stirring continuously for 5 minutes, until well heated. Add the cooked rice and continue for a further 8 to 10 minutes until piping hot. Add the peas. Taste and adjust the seasonings.

Whisk the egg with 1 × 15 ml spoon (1 tablespoon) water and a pinch of salt. Melt the remaining butter in a frying pan, pour in the egg mixture and cook, without stirring, until set. Turn out and cut into narrow strips. Turn the pork mixture into a hot serving dish and garnish with the strips of omelette.

Eskdale pork

Metric	Imperial
50 g fresh breadcrumbs	2 oz fresh breadcrumbs
75 g salami, diced	3 oz salami, diced
Finely grated rind and juice of 1 small orange	Finely grated rind and juice of 1 small orange
1 × 15 ml spoon finely chopped parsley	1 tablespoon finely chopped parsley
1 × 5 ml spoon dried thyme	1 teaspoon dried thyme
Salt and freshly ground black pepper	Salt and freshly ground black pepper
1 egg, beaten	1 egg, beaten
1¼ kg piece lean belly pork, boned and scored	2½ lb piece lean belly pork, boned and scored
A little oil	A little oil
1 × 15 ml spoon flour	1 tablespoon flour
300 ml stock	½ pint stock
1 × 5 ml spoon tomato purée	1 teaspoon tomato purée
To garnish:	To garnish:
Orange slices	Orange slices
Fresh parsley	Fresh parsley
Salami cones	Salami cones

Cooking Time: about 2 hours.
Oven: 190°C, 375°F, Gas Mark 5.

Combine the breadcrumbs, salami, orange rind, parsley, thyme and seasonings and bind together with the egg. Trim the pork, removing any gristle or bone. Spread the stuffing over the inside of the pork and roll up to enclose the stuffing. Secure with skewers and fine string. Place in a roasting tin and rub the skin lightly with oil, then rub with salt. Cook in a moderately hot oven for about 2 hours until well browned, crispy and cooked through. Baste once or twice during cooking and roast potatoes alongside the joint. Remove meat and keep warm. Use the pan drippings and the flour, stock, orange juice, tomato purée and seasonings to make a gravy.

Garnish pork with orange slices, parsley and salami cones, and serve with roast potatoes.
Serves 6.

Military pork jalousie

Metric	Imperial
40 g butter	1½ oz butter
1 small onion, peeled and chopped	1 small onion, peeled and chopped
40 g flour	1½ oz flour
300 ml stock or milk	½ pint stock or milk
Salt and freshly ground black pepper	Salt and freshly ground black pepper
2 × 15 ml spoons Military or other chunky pickle	2 tablespoons Military or other chunky pickle
350 g lean cooked pork, finely chopped	12 oz lean cooked pork, finely chopped
368 g packet frozen puff pastry, thawed	13 oz packet frozen puff pastry, thawed
Beaten egg to glaze	Beaten egg to glaze
To garnish:	To garnish:
Mustard and cress	Mustard and cress

Cooking time: about 50 minutes.
Oven: 220°C, 425°F, Gas Mark 7.
       190°C, 375°F, Gas Mark 5.

Melt the butter in a pan and fry the onion until soft. Stir in the flour and cook for 1 minute. Gradually add the stock or milk and bring to the boil, stirring continuously. Season, add the pickle and pork and simmer gently for 4–5 minutes. Taste and adjust the seasonings and leave to cool.
Roll out the pastry and cut into two pieces 28 cm × 15 cm (11 in × 6 in). Place one on a dampened baking sheet and spread the filling over the pastry leaving a 2·5 cm (1 in) margin all round. Brush the border with water. Roll the other piece out to 30 cm × 18 cm (12 in × 7 in) then fold in half lengthwise and cut into the fold at 1 cm (½ in) intervals to within 2·5 cm (1 in) of the edge, leaving 5 cm (2 in) at each end. Unfold the pastry, placing it carefully over the filling. Press the edges well together and 'knock up' with a knife. Brush the pastry all over with beaten egg.
Cook in a hot oven for about 15 minutes then reduce oven temperature to moderately hot and continue for a further 20 to 25 minutes until well risen and golden brown. Serve hot or cold, garnished with mustard and cress.
Note: other cold meats can be used in place of pork.

Eskdale pork; Military pork jalousie; Pork and liver terrine

Pork and liver terrine

Metric

350 g lean belly pork,
skinned
225 g pigs' or lambs' liver
25 g butter
1 onion, peeled
1–2 cloves garlic, crushed
1 × 15 ml spoon capers
25 g fresh breadcrumbs
Salt and freshly ground
black pepper
1 large egg, beaten
3 × 15 ml spoons stock

To garnish:

Few cucumber slices
6–8 stuffed olives
150 ml aspic jelly

Imperial

12 oz lean belly pork,
skinned
8 oz pigs' or lambs' liver
1 oz butter
1 onion, peeled
1–2 cloves garlic, crushed
1 tablespoon capers
1 oz fresh breadcrumbs
Salt and freshly ground
black pepper
1 large egg, beaten
3 tablespoons stock

To garnish:

Few cucumber slices
6–8 stuffed olives
¼ pint aspic jelly

Cooking Time: about 1¾ hours.
Oven: 160°C, 325°F, Gas Mark 3.

Roughly chop the pork and liver and fry in the melted butter for 10 minutes, stirring occasionally. Cool slightly, then mince finely with the onion, garlic and capers. Add the breadcrumbs, seasonings, egg and stock and press into a greased 15 cm (6 in) round ovenproof dish. Stand in a baking tin containing 4 cm (1½ in) water, cover with buttered paper and cook in a warm oven for 1½–1¾ hours, until cooked through.

Remove and cool, then chill thoroughly.

Decorate the top with cucumber and sliced stuffed olives and spoon over a thin layer of aspic. Chill until set.

Serves 4–6.

Tomato baked bacon

Metric	Imperial
1½ kg prime collar joint bacon	3 lb prime collar joint bacon
16–20 cloves	16–20 cloves
350 g button onions, peeled	12 oz button onions, peeled
15 g butter	½ oz butter
450 g tomatoes, peeled and quartered	1 lb tomatoes, peeled and quartered
1 × 5 ml spoon basil	1 teaspoon basil
150 ml dry white wine	¼ pint dry white wine
2 × 15 ml spoons breadcrumbs	2 tablespoons breadcrumbs
Salt and freshly ground black pepper	Salt and freshly ground black pepper

Cooking Time: 2 hours.
Oven: 190°C, 375°F, Gas Mark 5.

Place the joint in a saucepan and cover with cold water. Bring to the boil and simmer for an hour. Drain and remove the skin and place the bacon in an ovenproof casserole. Stud the fat with cloves.

Fry the onions in melted butter until browned and arrange around the joint. Add the tomatoes to the casserole, sprinkle with basil and add the wine. Cover and cook in a moderately hot oven for 35 to 40 minutes, until tender.

Remove the lid, sprinkle the breadcrumbs over the fat and return to the oven for 10 minutes. Taste the juices and adjust seasonings before serving.
Serves 6.

Bacon hotpot

Metric	Imperial
1 kg forehock of bacon joint, boned and rolled	2 lb forehock of bacon joint, boned and rolled
4–6 leeks, cleaned and sliced	4–6 leeks, cleaned and sliced
25 g butter	1 oz butter
4 carrots, peeled and sliced	4 carrots, peeled and sliced
450 g potatoes, peeled and thinly sliced	1 lb potatoes, peeled and thinly sliced
Salt and freshly ground black pepper	Salt and freshly ground black pepper
300 ml ham stock	½ pint ham stock

Cooking Time: about 2½ hours.
Oven: 190°C, 375°F, Gas Mark 5.

Soak the bacon in cold water for several hours then drain and place in a saucepan and cover with fresh cold water. Bring to the boil, remove the scum, cover and simmer gently for 1 hour. Remove from the saucepan, strip off the skin and cut into 2·5 cm (1 in) cubes.

Fry the leeks gently in butter for 5 minutes then layer with the carrots, potatoes and bacon in an ovenproof casserole, finishing with a layer of potato. Season the stock and pour into the casserole. Cover and cook in a moderately hot oven, for 45 minutes, then remove the lid and continue for a further 20 to 30 minutes, until tender.

Note: half the stock can be replaced with sweet cider if preferred.

Quick bacon pizza

Metric	Imperial
200 g self-raising flour	8 oz self-raising flour
Salt and freshly ground black pepper	Salt and freshly ground black pepper
50 g butter or margarine	2 oz butter or margarine
1 × 15 ml spoon finely chopped parsley or oregano	1 tablespoon finely chopped parsley or oregano
1 egg, beaten	1 egg, beaten
A little milk to mix	A little milk to mix
226 g can peeled tomatoes, partly drained	8 oz can peeled tomatoes, partly drained
225 g streaky bacon rashers, derinded and lightly fried	8 oz streaky bacon rashers, derinded and lightly fried
100 g English Mature Cheddar cheese, grated	4 oz English Mature Cheddar cheese, grated
½ × 65 g can anchovies, drained	½ × 2½ oz can anchovies, drained
8 stuffed olives, halved	8 stuffed olives, halved

Cooking Time: about 30 minutes.
Oven: 230°C, 450°F, Gas Mark 8.

Sieve the flour into a bowl with the seasonings. Add the fat and rub in until the mixture resembles fine breadcrumbs. Add the herbs and egg and sufficient milk to mix to a fairly soft dough. Knead lightly and shape into a 20 cm (8 in) round. Slide on to a lightly greased baking sheet. Spoon the tomatoes on top, breaking them up a little, and cover with the halved bacon rashers. Cook the pizza for 15 minutes in a very hot oven.

Remove from the oven, cover with cheese and arrange the anchovies and olives on top in a lattice pattern. Return to the oven for 5 to 10 minutes until the cheese is bubbling. Serve hot.

Tomato baked bacon; Bacon hotpot; Quick bacon pizza

Bacon chops with prunes

Metric

4 thick bacon chops
50–100 g large prunes,
soaked
1 large cooking apple,
peeled, cored and thinly
sliced

To garnish:
25 g butter
2 cooking apples, cored
and cut into rings
Parsley sprigs

Imperial

4 thick bacon chops
2–4 oz large prunes,
soaked
1 large cooking apple,
peeled, cored and thinly
sliced

To garnish:
1 oz butter
2 cooking apples, cored
and cut into rings
Parsley sprigs

Cooking Time: about 20 minutes.

Trim off the rind and cut a deep 'pocket' through the fat into the 'eye' of each bacon chop. Remove the stones from the prunes and chop roughly. Mix with the apple and use to fill the pockets. Secure with wooden cocktail sticks. Place on a grill rack and cook under a moderate heat for 5 to 7 minutes each side until cooked through. Keep warm.
Melt the butter and fry the apple rings until golden brown. Arrange apple rings on top of the chops and garnish with parsley sprigs.

Bacon and onion pudding; Bacon with sage and onion sauce

Bacon chops with prunes

Bacon and onion pudding

Metric

200 g self-raising flour
½ teaspoon salt
75 g shredded suet
1 × 5 ml spoon mixed
herbs
Water to mix

Filling:
550 g piece of lean bacon,
derinded and diced
Freshly ground black
pepper
2 onions, peeled and
sliced
4 × 15 ml spoons stock
or water

Imperial

8 oz self-raising flour
½ teaspoon salt
3 oz shredded suet
1 teaspoon mixed herbs
Water to mix

Filling:
1¼ lb piece of lean bacon,
derinded and diced
Freshly ground black
pepper
2 onions, peeled and
sliced
4 tablespoons stock or
water

Cooking Time: 4 hours.

Put a large saucepan of water to boil and thoroughly grease a 1 litre (2 pint) pudding basin.

Sieve the flour and salt into a bowl. Mix in the suet and herbs and mix to a soft dough with water. Cut off a quarter of the pastry for the lid and roll the remainder into a circle about twice the diameter of the top of the basin. Carefully lower the circle into the basin and press to the sides without tearing or creasing.

Season the bacon with pepper only and mix with the onions. Place in the pastry lined basin and add the stock. Roll out the remaining pastry for the lid, dampen the edges and place on top of the meat. Press the edges well together and trim. Cover securely with greased paper and then foil or a pudding cloth. Lower the basin into the pan so that the water comes half to two-thirds of the way up the side of the basin. Simmer gently for 4 hours, filling up the pan with more boiling water as necessary.

Remove the coverings and serve straight from the basin.

Bacon with sage and onion sauce

Metric

2 bacon knuckles
2 × 5 ml spoons sugar
1 bay leaf
50 g butter
2 onions, peeled and
thinly sliced
50 g flour
450 ml milk
150 ml cooking liquor
Salt and freshly ground
black pepper
2–3 × 5 ml spoons dried
sage

Imperial

2 bacon knuckles
2 teaspoons sugar
1 bay leaf
2 oz butter
2 onions, peeled and
thinly sliced
2 oz flour
¾ pint milk
¼ pint cooking liquor
Salt and freshly ground
black pepper
2–3 teaspoons dried
sage

Cooking Time: about 1½ hours.

Put the bacon knuckles into a saucepan and just cover with water. Add the sugar and bay leaf and bring to the boil. Remove the scum, cover and simmer for 1½ hours or until the bacon is tender.

To make the sauce, melt the butter in a pan and fry the onions very gently until soft but not coloured, stir in the flour and cook for 1 minute then gradually add the milk and bring to the boil. Add sufficient cooking liquor to give the required consistency. Season to taste, add the sage and simmer for 3 to 4 minutes.

Remove the skin from the knuckles, strip the meat off the bone and arrange on a hot serving dish. Either pour the sauce over the bacon or serve separately in a sauce boat.

Pickled bacon puffs

Metric	Imperial
40 g butter	1½ oz butter
1 small onion, peeled and finely chopped	1 small onion, peeled and finely chopped
50 g mushrooms, cleaned, trimmed and chopped	2 oz mushrooms, cleaned, trimmed and chopped
25 g flour	1 oz flour
150 ml chicken stock	¼ pint chicken stock
4 × 15 ml spoons milk	4 tablespoons milk
Salt and freshly ground black pepper	Salt and freshly ground black pepper
175 g cooked ham, finely chopped	6 oz cooked ham, finely chopped
3 pickled walnuts, chopped	3 pickled walnuts, chopped
225 g frozen puff pastry, thawed	8 oz frozen puff pastry, thawed
Beaten egg to glaze	Beaten egg to glaze
To garnish:	To garnish:
Watercress sprigs	Watercress sprigs

Cooking Time: 35–40 minutes.
Oven: 220°C, 425°F, Gas Mark 7.

Melt the butter in a pan and fry the onion and mushrooms gently until soft. Stir in the flour and cook for 1 minute then gradually add the stock and milk and bring to the boil, stirring frequently. Simmer for 3 minutes then season to taste and stir in the ham and the pickled walnuts and leave the filling to cool.

Roll out one-third of the pastry thinly and cut into four 13 cm (5 in) circles. Place on a dampened baking sheet and spoon the filling on to the pastry leaving a 1·5 cm (½ in) margin all round. Roll out the remaining pastry and cut into four 15 cm (6 in) rounds. Brush the pastry margins with water and position the lids. Press the edges very well together, then 'knock up' the edges and crimp. Make 2 slits in the top of each puff and decorate with the pastry trimmings.

Brush with beaten egg and cook in a hot oven for about 25 minutes until the pastry is well risen and golden brown. Serve the pickled bacon puffs hot or cold, garnished with watercress.

Bacon and cheese slice

Metric	Imperial
25 g butter	1 oz butter
25 g flour	1 oz flour
250 ml milk	8 fl oz milk
1 × 5 ml spoon made mustard	1 teaspoon made mustard
75 g English Mature Cheddar cheese, grated	3 oz English Mature Cheddar cheese, grated
Salt and freshly ground black pepper	Salt and freshly ground black pepper
225 g cooked ham or bacon, finely chopped	8 oz cooked ham or bacon, finely chopped
4 stuffed olives, sliced	4 stuffed olives, sliced
Pastry:	Pastry:
200 g plain flour	8 oz plain flour
Pinch of salt	Pinch of salt
50 g margarine	2 oz margarine
50 g lard or white fat	2 oz lard or white fat
Water to mix	Water to mix
2 hard-boiled eggs, thickly sliced	2 hard-boiled eggs, thickly sliced
Beaten egg or milk to glaze	Beaten egg or milk to glaze
To garnish:	To garnish:
Cucumber slices	Cucumber slices

Cooking Time: about 40 minutes.
Oven: 220°C, 425°F, Gas Mark 7.
180°C, 350°F, Gas Mark 4.

Melt the butter in a pan, stir in the flour and cook for 1 minute. Gradually add the milk and bring to the boil, stirring continuously. Simmer for 3 minutes then stir in the mustard and cheese and season to taste; add the ham or bacon and the stuffed olives and leave the filling to cool.

Sieve the flour with a pinch of salt into a bowl. Add the fats and rub in until the mixture resembles fine breadcrumbs. Add sufficient water to bind to a pliable dough. Turn out on to a floured surface and roll out thinly to a 30 cm (12 in) square. Place half the filling down the centre of the pastry, lay the eggs on top and cover with the remaining filling. Cut the sides of the pastry into diagonal strips 2 cm (¾ in) wide and plait these pieces evenly to enclose the filling completely. Transfer to a dampened baking sheet and brush the top with egg or milk. Cook in a hot oven for 20 minutes then reduce oven temperature to moderate and continue for a further 15 to 20 minutes until the pastry is golden brown. Serve hot or cold. Garnish with slices of cucumber.

Bacon toad; Bacon and cheese slice; Pickled bacon puffs

Bacon toad

Metric

450 g collar bacon
1 onion, peeled
1–2 × 5 ml spoons mixed herbs
Salt and freshly ground black pepper
3 eggs
Fat for cooking
100 g plain flour
250 ml milk

Sauce:
25 g butter
25 g flour
Pinch of salt
300 ml milk
2 × 15 ml spoons finely chopped parsley (optional)

Imperial

1 lb collar bacon
1 onion, peeled
1–2 teaspoons mixed herbs
Salt and freshly ground black pepper
3 eggs
Fat for cooking
4 oz plain flour
½ pint milk

Sauce:
1 oz butter
1 oz flour
Pinch of salt
½ pint milk
2 tablespoons finely chopped parsley (optional)

Cooking Time: about 1 hour.
Oven: 220°C, 425°F, Gas Mark 7.

Remove the rind and any bone or gristle from the bacon and mince with the onion. Add the herbs and seasonings and bind together with 1 beaten egg. Divide into 16 and shape into small balls. Fry these balls quickly in a little fat until lightly browned all over.

To make the batter, sieve the flour with a pinch of salt into a bowl, make a well in the centre, add the 2 eggs and gradually beat in the milk to give a smooth batter.

Heat 1 × 15 ml spoon (1 tablespoon) fat in a baking tin approx 28 × 23 cm (11 × 9 in) making sure the whole tin is coated. Add the bacon balls and cook in a hot oven for 5 minutes. Pour the batter into the tin and cook for 30 to 40 minutes or until well risen and golden brown.

Meanwhile, to make the sauce, melt the butter in a pan. Stir in the flour and cook for 1 minute, then gradually add the milk and bring to the boil, stirring continuously. Season to taste, add the parsley and simmer for 3 minutes. Serve the sauce with the bacon toad.

Savoury bacon pie

Metric

25 g butter
1 large onion, peeled
and chopped
225 g plain flour
300 ml milk
Salt and freshly ground
black pepper
½ teaspoon spoon
Worcestershire sauce
½–1 × 5 ml spoon mixed
herbs
175 g cooked ham or
bacon, chopped
50 g margarine
50 g lard or white fat
Water to mix
2 hard-boiled eggs, sliced
2 large tomatoes, peeled
and sliced
Beaten egg or milk to
glaze

Imperial

1 oz butter
1 large onion, peeled
and chopped
9 oz plain flour
½ pint milk
Salt and freshly ground
black pepper
½ teaspoon Worcestershire
sauce
½–1 teaspoon mixed
herbs
6 oz cooked ham or
bacon, chopped
2 oz margarine
2 oz lard or white fat
Water to mix
2 hard-boiled eggs, sliced
2 large tomatoes, peeled
and sliced
Beaten egg or milk to
glaze

Cooking Time: about 1 hour.
Oven: 220°C, 425°F, Gas Mark 7.
180°C, 350°F, Gas Mark 4.

Melt the butter in a pan and fry the onion until soft. Stir in 25 g (1 oz) flour and cook for 1 minute then gradually add the milk and bring to the boil. Season well, add the Worcestershire sauce and herbs and simmer for 3 minutes. Stir in the ham, taste and adjust the seasonings and cool. Sieve the remaining flour with a pinch of salt into a bowl, add the fats and rub in until the mixture resembles fine breadcrumbs. Add sufficient water to mix to a pliable dough. On a floured surface roll out two-thirds of the pastry and use to line a 20 cm (8 in) pie plate or tin. Spoon half the filling into the pastry, cover with the eggs and then the remaining filling. Lay the tomatoes on top. Roll out the remaining pastry for a lid, damp the edges, put in position and trim off the excess pastry. Press the edges well together and crimp. Make a hole in the centre of the lid and decorate around it with pastry trimmings.
Brush with egg or milk and cook in a hot oven for 20 minutes, then reduce oven temperature to moderate and continue for 20 to 25 minutes until the pastry is golden brown. Serve hot or cold.

Gammon with peaches

Metric

425 g can peach halves
1 × 15 ml spoon grated
onion
1 × 15 ml spoon finely
chopped parsley
Salt and freshly ground
black pepper
A little ground cinnamon
40 g fresh breadcrumbs
4 thin gammon slices
1 × 15 ml spoon lemon
juice
½ teaspoon dry mustard
mustard
20 whole cloves
2 × 15 ml spoons
demerara sugar
To garnish:
Watercress sprigs

Imperial

15 oz can peach halves
1 tablespoon grated
onion
1 tablespoon finely
chopped parsley
Salt and freshly ground
black pepper
A little ground cinnamon
1½ oz fresh breadcrumbs
4 thin gammon slices
1 tablespoon lemon juice
½ teaspoon dry mustard
20 whole cloves
2 tablespoons demerara
sugar
To garnish:
Watercress sprigs

Cooking Time: about 50 minutes.
Oven: 180°C, 350°F, Gas Mark 4.

Reserve four peach halves for garnish and finely chop the remainder. Mix with the onion, parsley, seasonings, cinnamon and breadcrumbs and bind together with a little peach juice.
Divide the stuffing mixture between the gammon placing it in the centre of each slice. Fold over to enclose completely and secure with wooden cocktail sticks, if necessary. Place in a shallow ovenproof dish. Combine 150 ml (¼ pint) peach juice with the lemon juice, mustard and a little black pepper. Pour over the gammon and cook, uncovered, in a moderate oven for 40 minutes.
Baste the gammon and place a peach half studded with cloves on each roll or arranged at either end of the serving dish. Sprinkle with sugar and return to the oven for 10 minutes before serving garnished with watercress sprigs.

Savoury bacon pie; Gammon with peaches; Ham mousse

Ham mousse

Metric

40 g caster sugar
1 × 15 ml spoon dry
mustard
½ teaspoon salt
Freshly ground black
pepper
3 large eggs, beaten
6 × 15 ml spoons wine
vinegar
1 × 15 ml spoon powdered
gelatine (15 g packet)
2 × 15 ml spoons water
150 ml double cream
1 × 15 ml spoon creamed
horseradish
350 g cooked ham, finely
chopped or minced

To garnish:
Cooked asparagus

Imperial

1½ oz caster sugar
1 tablespoon dry
mustard
½ teaspoon salt
Freshly ground black
pepper
3 large eggs, beaten
6 tablespoons wine
vinegar
1 tablespoon
powdered gelatine (½ oz
packet)
2 tablespoons water
¼ pint double cream
1 tablespoon creamed
horseradish
12 oz cooked ham, finely
chopped or minced

To garnish:
Cooked asparagus

Cooking Time: about 5 minutes.

Mix together the sugar, dry mustard, salt, pepper and eggs. Bring the vinegar to the boil and whisk into the egg mixture. Return to the pan and cook over a very gentle heat until thickened, stirring continuously. Do not boil or the sauce will curdle.

Dissolve the gelatine in the water in a small basin over a pan of hot water, cool slightly then add to the sauce. Cool, then stir in the cream, horseradish and ham. Pour into a well greased 900 ml (1½ pint) fluted mould and chill until set. Turn out on to a serving dish and garnish with the asparagus before serving.

55

Ham and chicory au gratin

Metric

4 large or 8 small heads
of chicory
8 thin slices cooked ham
English mustard
175 g English Mature
Cheddar cheese, grated
40 g butter
40 g flour
300 ml milk
150 ml dry cider or milk
Salt and freshly ground
black pepper
2 × 15 ml spoons fresh
breadcrumbs

Imperial

4 large or 8 small heads
of chicory
8 thin slices cooked ham
English mustard
6 oz English Mature
Cheddar cheese, grated
1½ oz butter
1½ oz flour
½ pint milk
¼ pint dry cider or milk
Salt and freshly ground
black pepper
2 tablespoons fresh
breadcrumbs

Cooking Time: about 50 minutes.
Oven: 220°C, 425°F, Gas Mark 7.

Trim the chicory and blanch in boiling water for 3 minutes. Drain and cut large heads in half lengthwise. Spread the ham lightly with mustard, sprinkle with 50 g (2 oz) of the cheese and place a piece of chicory on each slice. Roll up the ham slices tightly and place in a lightly greased shallow ovenproof dish.

Melt the butter in a pan, stir in the flour and cook for 1 minute. Gradually add the milk, and cider (if using) and bring to the boil, stirring continuously. Season well to taste and simmer for 3 minutes. Stir in 75 g (3 oz) of the cheese until melted then pour over the ham rolls.

Mix the remaining cheese with the breadcrumbs and sprinkle over the sauce. Cook in a hot oven for 30 to 40 minutes until well browned.

Ham and chicory au gratin

Glazed gammon

Metric	Imperial
1¾–2 kg gammon or prime collar joint	4 lb gammon or prime collar joint
4 cloves	4 cloves
1 bay leaf	1 bay leaf
100 g demerara sugar	4 oz demerara sugar
2 × 15 ml spoons wine vinegar	2 tablespoons wine vinegar
1 × 15 ml spoon honey	1 tablespoon honey

Cooking Time: about 2 hours. Oven: 180°C, 350°F, Gas Mark 4.

Weigh the joint and calculate the cooking time, allowing 20–25 minutes per 450 g (1 lb), plus 25 minutes over (depending on thickness of joint). Place in a saucepan and cover with water. Add the cloves, bay leaf and 25 g (1 oz) sugar and bring to the boil. Remove scum, cover and simmer gently for half the total cooking time. Drain the joint, wrap in foil and cook in a moderate oven until 30 minutes before the end of the total cooking time.

Unwrap foil, strip off the skin and score the fat into diamonds. Heat the vinegar and honey together and brush over the fat. Sprinkle with the remaining sugar, pressing it well in, and return to the oven for the remaining cooking time. Serve hot or cold.

Note: the joint can be soaked for 2–6 hours before cooking.

Glazed gammon

Orange stuffed veal roast

Metric	Imperial
1¼–1½ kg boned and rolled shoulder of veal	2½–3 lb boned and rolled shoulder of veal
Salt and freshly ground black pepper	Salt and freshly ground black pepper
1 cooking apple, peeled, cored and chopped	1 cooking apple, peeled, cored and chopped
1 small onion, peeled and finely chopped	1 small onion, peeled and finely chopped
Grated rind of 1 orange	Grated rind of 1 orange
Flesh of 2 oranges, diced	Flesh of 2 oranges, diced
50 g fresh breadcrumbs	2 oz fresh breadcrumbs
1 × 15 ml spoon finely chopped parsley	1 tablespoon finely chopped parsley
1 egg, beaten	1 egg, beaten
6 rashers streaky bacon	6 rashers streaky bacon
Dripping	Dripping
To garnish:	To garnish:
Glazed orange slices	Glazed orange slices

Cooking Time: 2–2½ hours.
Oven: 220°C, 425°F, Gas Mark 7.

Open out the joint and season the inside lightly. Combine the apple, onion, orange rind and flesh, breadcrumbs, parsley and seasonings, and bind together with the egg. Spread over the veal, roll up and secure with skewers and string. Weigh the joint and place in a roasting tin. Lay the bacon over the joint and spread liberally with dripping. Cook in a hot oven, allowing 30 minutes per 450 g (1 lb), plus 30 minutes over, and basting the joint every 15 minutes for the first 1½ hours. Cover the meat tightly with foil and continue for the remaining cooking time.

Serve the joint garnished with glazed orange slices and with a thin gravy made from the pan juices and if liked parsley for colour.

Note: to glaze orange slices, place them in the roasting tin alongside the joint for the last 15 minutes.
Serves 6.

Saltimbocca

Metric	Imperial
8 small, very thin slices of veal	8 small, very thin slices of veal
1 × 15 ml spoon lemon juice	1 tablespoon lemon juice
Salt and freshly ground black pepper	Salt and freshly ground black pepper
8 fresh sage leaves or a little dried sage	8 fresh sage leaves or a little dried sage
8 small, thin slices prosciutto or ham	8 small, thin slices prosciutto or ham
40 g butter	1½ oz butter
3–4 × 15 ml spoons Marsala	3–4 tablespoons Marsala
To garnish:	To garnish:
Croûtons	Croûtons
Sage leaves	Sage leaves

Cooking Time: about 30 minutes.

Ask the butcher to flatten the veal, or place the pieces between two sheets of waxed paper and beat flat with a mallet or chopper. Rub each piece with lemon juice and season lightly. Lay a sage leaf on each piece or sprinkle it with a little dried sage. Cover with prosciutto or cooked ham. Roll up and secure with wooden cocktail sticks.

Melt the butter in a pan and fry the rolls gently until golden brown all over. Add the Marsala and bring to the boil. Cover and simmer gently for about 20 minutes, or until tender. Taste and adjust the seasonings and serve with the juices poured over and garnished with croûtons and sage leaves.

Pot roast veal provençale

Metric	Imperial
1¼ kg shoulder of veal, boned and rolled	2½ lb shoulder of veal, boned and rolled
1 × 15 ml spoon dripping	1 tablespoon dripping
Salt and freshly ground black pepper	Salt and freshly ground black pepper
1 large onion, peeled and sliced	1 large onion, peeled and sliced
1 × 15 ml spoon tomato purée	1 tablespoon tomato purée
396 g can peeled tomatoes	14 oz can peeled tomatoes
150 ml dry white wine	¼ pint dry white wine
Good pinch of sugar	Good pinch of sugar
A little garlic powder or crushed garlic	A little garlic powder or crushed garlic

Cooking Time: about 2 hours.
Oven: 190°C, 375°F, Gas Mark 5.

Brown the joint all over in melted dripping; season lightly and place in an ovenproof casserole.

Fry the onion in the same fat until soft, add the tomato purée, canned tomatoes and wine and bring to the boil. Season well, add the sugar and pour over the veal. Sprinkle the outside of the veal with garlic and cover the casserole tightly. Cook in a moderately hot oven for 1 hour.

Baste well then continue for a further hour or until tender. Taste and adjust the seasonings. To serve slice the veal, surround with the sauce and garnish with parsley, if liked. Serves 5–6.

Pot roast veal provençal; Saltimbocca; Orange stuffed veal roast

Veal croquettes with mushroom sauce; Creamy veal olives; Vitello tonnato

Veal croquettes with mushroom sauce

Metric

350 g lean pie veal
1 onion, peeled
225 g fresh sausagemeat
Salt and freshly ground
black pepper
Tabasco sauce
¼ teaspoon ground mace
1 egg, beaten
Fresh breadcrumbs for
coating
Fat for frying
25 g butter
1 onion, peeled and
finely sliced

Sauce:
100 g mushrooms, cleaned,
trimmed and sliced
300 ml stock
2 × 5 ml spoons cornflour
3 × 15 ml spoons soured
cream (optional)

Imperial

12 oz lean pie veal
1 onion, peeled
8 oz fresh sausagemeat
Salt and freshly ground
black pepper
Tabasco sauce
¼ teaspoon ground mace
1 egg, beaten
Fresh breadcrumbs for
coating
Fat for frying
1 oz butter
1 onion, peeled and finely
sliced

Sauce:
4 oz mushrooms, cleaned,
trimmed and sliced
½ pint stock
2 teaspoons cornflour
3 tablespoons soured
cream (optional)

Cooking Time: about 30 minutes.

Finely mince the veal and onion and mix with the sausage-meat, seasonings, a dash of Tabasco, mace and half the beaten egg. Divide into four and form into flat triangle shapes. Dip in beaten egg and coat in breadcrumbs; then fry gently in shallow fat for 10 to 12 minutes each side, until cooked through and well browned. Drain the croquettes on absorbent kitchen paper and keep warm.

Meanwhile, to make the sauce, fry the onion in butter until soft then add the mushrooms and continue for 2 to 3 minutes. Add the stock, seasonings and a good dash of Tabasco sauce and bring to the boil. Simmer the sauce for 10 minutes then thicken with the cornflour, blended in a little cold water, and return to the boil for 2 minutes.

Taste and adjust the seasonings and stir in the soured cream (if using). Reheat gently and serve with the croquettes.

Creamy veal olives

Metric	Imperial
4 small escalopes of veal, beaten flat	4 small escalopes of veal, beaten flat
Salt and freshly ground black pepper	Salt and freshly ground black pepper
2 slices cooked ham, halved	2 slices cooked ham, halved
2 large eggs, hard-boiled and halved	2 large eggs, hard-boiled and halved
50 g butter	2 oz butter
300 ml seasoned white stock	½ pint seasoned white stock
2 × 15 ml spoons dry white wine (optional)	2 tablespoons dry white wine (optional)
100 g button mushrooms, cleaned, trimmed and quartered	4 oz button mushrooms, cleaned, trimmed and quartered
20 g flour	¾ oz flour
4 × 15 ml spoons double cream	4 tablespoons double cream
To garnish:	To garnish:
Parsley	Parsley

Cooking Time: about 1¼ hours.
Oven: 180°C, 350°F, Gas Mark 4.

Trim the escalopes and season lightly. Place half a slice of ham and half an egg on each one; roll up and secure with wooden cocktail sticks. Heat 25 g/1 oz butter in a pan and fry the veal olives until browned all over. Transfer to a shallow ovenproof casserole. Pour on the stock and wine, cover and cook in a moderate oven for 1 hour. Drain off the liquor and reserve. Keep the olives warm.
Melt the remaining butter in a pan and fry the mushrooms gently for 2 minutes. Stir in the flour and cook for 1 minute. Gradually add the cooking liquor and bring to the boil. Season to taste and simmer for 2 minutes. Stir in the cream and reheat gently without boiling. Pour back over the olives and garnish with parsley.

Vitello tonnato

Metric	Imperial
675 g boned leg of veal, rolled	1½ lb boned leg of veal, rolled
1 bay leaf	1 bay leaf
6 peppercorns	6 peppercorns
1 carrot, peeled and sliced	1 carrot, peeled and sliced
1 onion, peeled and sliced	1 onion, peeled and sliced
2 sticks celery, scrubbed and chopped	2 sticks celery, scrubbed and chopped
Stock or water	Stock or water
65 g can tuna fish	2½ oz can tuna fish
1 can anchovy fillets, drained	1 can anchovy fillets, drained
150 ml olive oil	¼ pint olive oil
2 egg yolks	2 egg yolks
1 × 15 ml spoon lemon juice	1 tablespoon lemon juice
Salt and freshly ground black pepper	Salt and freshly ground black pepper
To garnish:	To garnish:
Capers	Capers
Lemon slices	Lemon slices
Parsley sprigs	Parsley sprigs

Cooking Time: about 1 hour.

Place the veal in a saucepan with the bay leaf, peppercorns, vegetables and sufficient stock to cover barely. Bring to the boil, remove the scum, cover and simmer gently for about 1 hour or until tender. Drain and cool.
Meanwhile thoroughly mash the tuna fish with 4 anchovy fillets and 1 × 15 ml spoon (1 tablespoon) oil, then add the egg yolks and either press through a sieve or liquidise until very smooth. Stir in the lemon juice and gradually beat in the remaining oil, a little at a time, until the sauce is smooth and has the consistency of thin cream. Season to taste.
Slice the veal thinly and arrange in a shallow dish. Spoon the sauce over to coat completely, cover the dish and chill overnight.
Before serving, garnish with the remaining anchovies, capers, lemon slices and parsley.
Serves 6.

Veal and lemon cobbler

Metric	Imperial
1 large onion, peeled and sliced	1 large onion, peeled and sliced
25 g butter	1 oz butter
1 × 15 ml spoon oil	1 tablespoon oil
675 g pie veal	1½ lb pie veal
25 g flour	1 oz flour
450 ml white stock	¾ pint white stock
Salt and freshly ground black pepper	Salt and freshly ground black pepper
Finely grated rind of 1 small lemon	Finely grated rind of 1 small lemon
1 × 15 ml spoon lemon juice	1 tablespoon lemon juice
100 g mushrooms, cleaned, trimmed and sliced	4 oz mushrooms, cleaned, trimmed and sliced
Scone topping:	Scone topping:
200 g self-raising flour	8 oz self-raising flour
A little salt and pepper	A little salt and pepper
50 g butter or margarine	2 oz butter or margarine
Finely grated rind of ½ small lemon	Finely grated rind of ½ small lemon
1 egg, beaten	1 egg, beaten
approx 4 × 15 ml spoons milk to mix and glaze	approx 4 tablespoons milk to mix and glaze

Cooking Time: about 1¾ hours.
Oven: 160°C, 325°F, Gas Mark 3.
    220°C, 425°F, Gas Mark 7.

Fry the onion in the butter and oil until soft, but not coloured, in a flameproof casserole. Trim the veal and cut into 2.5 cm (1 in) cubes, then add to the pan and fry for about 5 minutes until well sealed. Stir in the flour and cook for 1 minute then gradually add the stock and bring to the boil. Season well, add the lemon rind and juice and cover the casserole. Cook in a warm oven for 1¼ hours, or until tender. Stir the mushrooms into the casserole.

To make the topping, sift the flour and a little salt and pepper into a bowl. Rub in the fat until the mixture resembles fine breadcrumbs, then stir in the lemon rind. Add the egg and sufficient milk to mix to a fairly soft dough. Roll out to 1.5 cm (½ in) thickness on a floured surface and cut into 5 cm (2 in) rounds. Arrange these scones in an overlapping circle round the edge of the casserole to make a border on top of the veal. Brush with milk and cook in a hot oven for 10 to 15 minutes until well risen, golden brown and firm to the touch. Serve at once. Garnish with parsley, if liked.

Veal and lemon cobbler

Raised picnic pie

Metric	Imperial
350 g pie veal	12 oz pie veal
450 g cooked ham	1 lb cooked ham
1 small onion, peeled	1 small onion, peeled
Salt and freshly ground black pepper	Salt and freshly ground black pepper
Good pinch of ground mace	Good pinch of ground mace

Hot water pastry:	**Hot water pastry:**
110 g blended white vegetable fat	4½ oz blended white vegetable fat
150 ml water	¼ pint water
300 g plain flour	12 oz plain flour
1 egg, beaten	1 egg, beaten
2 × 5 ml spoons powdered gelatine	2 teaspoons powdered gelatine
300 ml stock	½ pint stock

To garnish:	**To garnish:**
Mixed salads	Mixed salads

Cooking Time: about 2 hours.
Oven: 200°C, 400°F, Gas Mark 6.
160°C, 325°F, Gas Mark 3.

Finely mince the veal with 100 g (4 oz) ham and the onion. Season well, add the mace and mix thoroughly. Cut remaining ham into thin strips.

To make the hot water pastry, melt the fat in the water and bring to the boil. Sieve the flour with ½ × 5 ml spoon (½ teaspoon) salt into a bowl. Add the boiling liquid and mix to a soft dough. Knead lightly then roll out three-quarters of the pastry and use to line an 18–20 cm (7–8 in) round, loose-bottomed cake tin, or a game pie mould. (Keep the remaining pastry covered in the bowl.) Place half the minced meat in the bottom, cover with strips of ham and then the remaining mince. Press down evenly. Roll out the remaining pastry for a lid, brush the edges with water and position. Press edges well together, trim and crimp. Decorate the top with pastry trimmings and make a hole in the centre. Brush with beaten egg and cook in a fairly hot oven for 30 minutes. Reduce oven temperature to warm and continue for 1¼–1½ hours, covering with foil when sufficiently browned.

Dissolve the gelatine in the stock and season well. As the pie cools, fill up with the stock through the central hole. Chill until firm then turn out and serve with mixed salads. Serves 6–8.

Raised picnic pie

Veal and spinach cannelloni; Cranberry glazed veal; Stuffed courgettes; Minted veal pie

Cranberry glazed veal

Metric

1½ kg shoulder of veal, boned and rolled, or loin of veal
Salt and freshly ground black pepper
1 onion, peeled and finely chopped
25 g butter
6 × 15 ml spoons cranberry sauce
6 × 15 ml spoons red wine
300 ml stock
1 × 15 ml spoon cornflour

To garnish:
Lattice potatoes
Bacon rolls
French beans (optional)

Imperial

3 lb shoulder of veal, boned and rolled, or loin of veal
Salt and freshly ground black pepper
1 onion, peeled and finely chopped
1 oz butter
6 tablespoons cranberry sauce
6 tablespoons red wine
½ pint stock
1 tablespoon cornflour

To garnish:
Lattice potatoes
Bacon rolls
French beans (optional)

Cooking Time: about 2 hours.
Oven: 220°C, 425°F, Gas Mark 7.

Lightly season the joint and place in a deep casserole. Fry the onion in the butter until soft. Add half the cranberry sauce and the wine and bring to the boil. Pour over the veal. Cook in a hot oven, allowing 30 minutes per 450 g (1 lb), plus 30 minutes over. Baste the joint every 15 minutes for the first 1½ hours. Spoon the remaining cranberry sauce over the joint, cover the casserole and continue to cook for the remaining time. Remove the joint to a serving dish and keep warm.

Spoon the fat from the juices in the casserole, add the stock and thicken with cornflour blended in a little cold water. Bring back to the boil for 2 minutes, taste and adjust the seasonings and serve with the veal. Garnish with potatoes, bacon rolls, and French beans, if liked.

Serves 6.

Veal and spinach cannelloni

Metric	Imperial
8 cannelloni	8 cannelloni
Salt and freshly ground black pepper	Salt and freshly ground black pepper
65 g butter	2½ oz butter
1 onion, peeled and chopped	1 onion, peeled and chopped
350 g pie veal, minced	12 oz pie veal, minced
225 g frozen chopped spinach, thawed	8 oz frozen chopped spinach, thawed
Pinch of nutmeg	Pinch of nutmeg
40 g flour	1½ oz flour
450 ml milk	¾ pint milk
75 g mature Cheddar cheese, grated	3 oz mature Cheddar cheese, grated

Cooking Time: about 1 hour.
Oven: 200°C, 400°F, Gas Mark 6.

Cook the cannelloni in boiling salted water according to the instructions on the packet. Drain well.
Melt 25 g (1 oz) butter in a pan and fry the onion until soft, stir in the veal and cook gently for 15 minutes, stirring frequently. Add the drained spinach, seasonings and nutmeg, cook for 10 minutes. Melt the remaining butter in a pan, stir in the flour, cook for 1 minute. Gradually add the milk and bring to the boil, stirring continuously. Season to taste and simmer for 3 minutes. Stir 150 ml (¼ pint) sauce into the veal mixture; taste and adjust seasonings.
Stuff the cannelloni with the veal and place in a greased shallow ovenproof dish. Add 50 g (2 oz) cheese to the remaining sauce and pour over the cannelloni. Sprinkle with the remaining cheese and cook in a moderately hot oven for about 30 minutes until golden brown and bubbling.

Stuffed courgettes

Metric	Imperial
1 small onion, peeled and chopped	1 small onion, peeled and chopped
25 g butter	1 oz butter
225 g raw minced veal	8 oz raw minced veal
25 g fresh breadcrumbs	1 oz fresh breadcrumbs
Salt and freshly ground black pepper	Salt and freshly ground black pepper
1 × 5 ml spoon finely chopped mint	1 teaspoon finely chopped mint
1 egg yolk	1 egg yolk
8 medium-sized courgettes	8 medium-sized courgettes
150 ml white stock	¼ pint white stock
225 g freshly boiled spaghetti	8 oz freshly boiled spaghetti
50 g mild Emmenthal cheese, finely grated	2 oz mild Emmenthal cheese, finely grated

Cooking Time: about 1 hour.
Oven: 180°C, 350°F, Gas Mark 4.

Fry the onion in the butter until soft then stir in the minced veal and cook gently for 10 minutes, stirring frequently. Remove from the heat and stir in the breadcrumbs, seasonings, mint and egg yolk.
Wash and trim the courgettes and cut in half lengthwise. Discard some of the seeds and fill each courgette with the veal mixture. Put the two halves back together and secure with cotton, or wooden cocktail sticks. Place in a lightly greased shallow ovenproof dish and pour the stock around. Cover and cook in a moderate oven for about 45 minutes until tender.
Remove the cotton or sticks and serve on a bed of boiled spaghetti, tossed in a little butter and seasoned, with the grated cheese handed separately in a bowl.

Minted veal pie

Metric	Imperial
450 g lean pie veal	1 lb lean pie veal
1 onion, peeled	1 onion, peeled
25 g butter	1 oz butter
50–100 g mushrooms, cleaned, trimmed and chopped	2–4 oz mushrooms, cleaned, trimmed and chopped
1 × 15 ml spoon flour	1 tablespoon flour
150 ml stock	¼ pint stock
2 × 5 ml spoons dried mint	2 teaspoons dried mint
Salt and freshly ground black pepper	Salt and freshly ground black pepper
200 g plain flour	8 oz plain flour
50 g margarine	2 oz margarine
50 g lard or white fat	2 oz lard or white fat
Water to mix	Water to mix
Milk to glaze	Milk to glaze

Cooking Time: about 1 hour.
Oven: 220°C, 425°F, Gas Mark 7.
180°C, 350°F, Gas Mark 4.

Mince the veal and onion coarsely. Cook gently in a pan with the butter for 10 minutes, stirring occasionally. Add the mushrooms and continue cooking for 2 minutes. Stir in the 1 × 15 ml (1 tablespoon) of flour, followed by the stock, mint and seasonings, and bring to the boil for 2 minutes. Taste and adjust the seasonings and cool.
Sieve the 200 g (8 oz) flour and a pinch of salt into a bowl, add the fats and rub in until the mixture resembles fine breadcrumbs. Add sufficient water to mix to a pliable dough. Roll out half the pastry, use to line a 20 cm (8 in) pie plate or shallow tin, and spoon in the filling. Roll out the remaining pastry and cut into about 28 4 cm (1½ in) rounds. Brush with milk and place in overlapping circles all over the filling to make a lid. Glaze again with milk and cook in a hot oven for 20 minutes. Reduce oven temperature to moderate and cook for a further 20 to 30 minutes, until browned.

Osso bucco

Osso bucco

Metric	Imperial
1 kg shin of veal	2 lb shin of veal
Salt and freshly ground black pepper	Salt and freshly ground black pepper
25 g butter	1 oz butter
1 × 15 ml spoon oil	1 tablespoon oil
1 large onion, peeled and chopped	1 large onion, peeled and chopped
4 sticks celery, scrubbed and sliced	4 sticks celery, scrubbed and sliced
2 large carrots, peeled and sliced	2 large carrots, peeled and sliced
150 ml dry white wine	$\frac{1}{4}$ pint dry white wine
1 × 5 ml lemon juice	1 teaspoon lemon juice
300 ml white stock	$\frac{1}{2}$ pint white stock
$\frac{1}{2}$ teaspoon dried rosemary	$\frac{1}{2}$ teaspoon dried rosemary
396 g can peeled tomatoes	14 oz can peeled tomatoes
2 × 5 ml spoons cornflour (optional)	2 teaspoons cornflour (optional)

Cooking Time: about 2 hours.

Ask the butcher to saw the veal into 4 pieces. Trim and season. Melt the butter in a pan, add the oil and fry the veal until browned all over. Remove from the pan.

Fry the onion, celery and carrots until just beginning to colour then pour off any excess fat from the pan. Add the wine and lemon juice and replace the veal. Bring to the boil, cover and simmer very gently for 45 minutes.

Add the stock, rosemary, tomatoes and seasonings. Bring back to the boil, cover and simmer for a further hour or until the meat is tender. If liked, thicken with the cornflour blended in a little cold water and boil for 2 minutes.

Taste and adjust seasonings, if necessary. Sprinkle with a mixture of lemon rind and chopped parsley before serving, if liked.

Kidneys à l'orange

Kidneys à l'orange

Metric

4 rashers streaky bacon, derinded and chopped
2 onions, peeled and thinly sliced
40 g butter
8–10 lambs' kidneys, skinned, halved and cored
2 × 15 ml spoons seasoned flour
½ teaspoon paprika
300 ml stock
Finely grated rind and juice of 1 large orange
Salt and freshly ground black pepper
2 × 5 ml spoons tomato purée

To garnish:
Orange wedges
Chopped parsley

Imperial

4 rashers streaky bacon, derinded and chopped
2 onions, peeled and thinly sliced
1½ oz butter
8–10 lambs' kidneys, skinned, halved and cored
2 tablespoons seasoned flour
½ teaspoon paprika
½ pint stock
Finely grated rind and juice of 1 large orange
Salt and freshly ground black pepper
2 teaspoons tomato purée

To garnish:
Orange wedges
Chopped parsley

Cooking Time: about 30 minutes.

Fry the bacon and onions in the butter until soft. Coat the kidneys in seasoned flour and add to the pan. Cook gently for 5 minutes, turning frequently until well sealed. Stir in the remaining flour and paprika, cook for 1 minute then gradually add the stock, orange rind and juice. Bring slowly to the boil, season well and add the tomato paste. Cover and simmer gently for about 20 minutes until tender, adding a little more stock during cooking, if necessary. Taste and adjust seasonings and serve garnished with orange wedges and chopped parsley.

Kidney and sausage casserole

Metric	Imperial
225 g chipolata sausages, halved	8 oz chipolata sausages, halved
25 g butter or margarine	1 oz butter or margarine
6–8 lambs' kidneys, skinned, halved and cored	6–8 lambs' kidneys, skinned, halved and cored
1 large onion, peeled and chopped, or 8 button onions, peeled	1 large onion, peeled and chopped, or 8 button onions, peeled
15 g flour	½ oz flour
300 ml stock	½ pint stock
4 × 15 ml spoons red wine or sherry (optional)	4 tablespoons red wine or sherry (optional)
Salt and freshly ground black pepper	Salt and freshly ground black pepper
½ teaspoon dried dill	½ teaspoon dried dill
675 g creamed potato	1½ lb creamed potato
Beaten egg or melted butter to glaze	Beaten egg or melted butter to glaze
To garnish:	To garnish:
Chopped parsley	Chopped parsley

Cooking Time: about 50 minutes.
Oven: 180°C, 350°F, Gas Mark 4.

Fry the chipolatas in the melted fat, until lightly browned, in a fireproof casserole. Remove from the pan. Fry the kidneys until well sealed, then remove. Fry the onion until soft then stir in the flour and cook for 1 minute. Gradually add the stock and wine or sherry and bring to the boil. Replace the sausages and kidneys, season well and add the herbs. Cover the casserole and cook in a moderate oven for 30 to 40 minutes, until tender.

Meanwhile, pipe the potato around a shallow heatproof dish, brush it with egg or melted butter and brown under a hot grill.

To serve, spoon the sausage and kidney mixture into the potato-lined dish and sprinkle with chopped parsley.

Kidneys portugaise

Metric	Imperial
3 × 15 ml spoons oil	3 tablespoons oil
2 onions, peeled and finely chopped	2 onions, peeled and finely chopped
2 cloves garlic, crushed	2 cloves garlic, crushed
1 large red pepper, washed, deseeded and chopped	1 large red pepper, washed, deseeded and chopped
2 × 15 ml spoons tomato purée	2 tablespoons tomato purée
396 g can peeled tomatoes, chopped	14 oz can peeled tomatoes, chopped
4 × 15 ml spoons beef stock or water	4 tablespoons beef stock or water
½ teaspoon Worcestershire sauce	½ teaspoon Worcestershire sauce
Dash of Tabasco sauce	Dash of Tabasco sauce
1 × 15 ml spoon lemon juice	1 tablespoon lemon juice
Salt and freshly ground black pepper	Salt and freshly ground black pepper
25 g butter	1 oz butter
8–10 lambs' kidneys, skinned, halved and cored	8–10 lambs' kidneys, skinned, halved and cored
To garnish:	To garnish:
Black olives	Black olives

Cooking Time: about 30 minutes.

Heat 2 × 15 ml spoons (2 tablespoons) oil in a pan, add the onions and garlic and fry gently until soft. Add the pepper and continue gently for 4 to 5 minutes. Stir in the tomato purée, tomatoes, stock, Worcestershire sauce, Tabasco, lemon juice and seasonings. Bring to the boil, cover and simmer gently for 15 minutes, stirring occasionally.

Meanwhile, heat the remaining oil and the butter in another pan. Add the kidneys and fry gently for 8 to 10 minutes, stirring frequently, until well sealed and almost cooked through. Add the tomato mixture, cover and simmer gently for a further 5 to 10 minutes. Taste and adjust seasonings. Serve with boiled rice and garnish with black olives.

Kidney and sausage casserole; Kidneys portugaise; Kidney pancakes

Kidney pancakes

Metric

Batter:
100 g plain flour
Pinch of salt
2 eggs
300 ml milk
Lard or oil for frying

Filling:
50 g butter
8–10 lambs' kidneys,
skinned, cored and
chopped
100 g mushrooms, cleaned,
trimmed and chopped
40 g flour
300 ml beef stock
Salt and freshly ground
black pepper
Good dash of
Worcestershire sauce
150 ml single cream
40 g flaked almonds,
toasted
A little melted butter

To garnish:
Parsley sprigs

Imperial

Batter:
4 oz plain flour
Pinch of salt
2 eggs
½ pint milk
Lard or oil for frying

Filling:
2 oz butter
8–10 lambs' kidneys,
skinned, cored and
chopped
4 oz mushrooms, cleaned,
trimmed and chopped
1½ oz flour
½ pint beef stock
Salt and freshly ground
black pepper
Good dash of
Worcestershire sauce
¼ pint single cream
1½ oz flaked almonds,
toasted
A little melted butter

To garnish:
Parsley sprigs

Cooking Time: 45 minutes.
Oven: 180°C, 350°F, Gas Mark 4.

To make the batter, sift the flour with a pinch of salt into a bowl and make a well in the centre, add the eggs and a little milk and mix to a smooth thick batter. Continue adding the milk and beat until smooth. Use to make 8 thin pancakes in a small greased frying pan. Stack up on a plate with foil between each and keep the pancakes warm.

For the filling, melt the butter in a pan and fry the kidneys for about 5 minutes until well sealed, add the mushrooms and continue for 2 to 3 minutes. Stir in the flour followed by the stock, seasonings and Worcestershire sauce. Bring to the boil, cover and simmer for about 10 minutes or until tender. Stir in the cream and half the almonds and reheat without boiling. Taste and adjust the seasonings. Divide the filling between the pancakes and roll up.

Place the pancakes in a lightly greased shallow ovenproof dish and brush with melted butter. Sprinkle with the remaining almonds, cover with foil and cook in a moderate oven for about 20 minutes, until piping hot. Garnish with parsley sprigs.

Kidney fritters with mustard sauce

Metric	Imperial
25 g butter	1 oz butter
125 g flour	5 oz flour
300 ml stock	½ pint stock
Salt and freshly ground black pepper	Salt and freshly ground black pepper
1 × 15 ml spoon wine vinegar	1 tablespoon wine vinegar
1 × 15 ml spoon French mustard	1 tablespoon French mustard
25–50 g stuffed olives, sliced	1–2 oz stuffed olives, sliced
10–12 lambs' kidneys, skinned, quartered and cored	10–12 lambs' kidneys, skinned, quartered and cored
Flour for coating	Flour for coating
1 large egg	1 large egg
150 ml milk	¼ pint milk
1 × 5 ml spoon oil	1 teaspoon oil
Deep fat for frying	Deep fat for frying
To garnish:	To garnish:
Tomato	Tomato
Mustard and cress	Mustard and cress

Cooking Time: about 30 minutes.

To make the sauce, melt the butter in a pan, stir in 25 g (1 oz) flour and cook for 1 minute, gradually add the stock and bring to the boil for 3 minutes, stirring frequently. Season to taste, stir in the vinegar and mustard and simmer for 2 minutes. Add the olives and keep warm.

Prepare the kidneys and coat in flour. Sieve the remaining flour with a pinch of salt into a bowl. Add the egg and sufficient milk to beat to a smooth batter, then beat in the remaining milk. Heat the fat to 180–190°C/350–375°F, or until a cube of bread browns in it in 20 seconds. Dip the pieces of kidney in the batter, a few at a time, then drop into the hot fat and cook for 4 to 5 minutes until golden brown and crispy. Drain the fritters on absorbent kitchen paper and keep warm.

Garnish with tomato and mustard and cress and serve with the sauce.

Liver risotto

Metric	Imperial
50 g butter	2 oz butter
2 large onions, peeled and chopped	2 large onions, peeled and chopped
2 rashers streaky bacon, derinded and chopped	2 rashers streaky bacon, derinded and chopped
350 g lambs' or pigs' liver, trimmed and cut into cubes	12 oz lambs' or pigs' liver, trimmed and cut into cubes
225 g long-grain rice	8 oz long-grain rice
100 g button mushrooms, cleaned, trimmed and quartered	4 oz button mushrooms, cleaned, trimmed and quartered
226 g can peeled tomatoes	8 oz can peeled tomatoes
½–1 × 5 ml spoon marjoram (optional)	½–1 teaspoon marjoram (optional)
600 ml beef stock	1 pint beef stock
Salt and freshly ground black pepper	Salt and freshly ground black pepper
100 g freshly cooked peas	4 oz freshly cooked peas
Parmesan cheese (optional)	Parmesan cheese (optional)

Cooking Time: about 45 minutes.

Melt the butter in a heavy based pan. Fry the onions, bacon and liver for about 5 minutes until they are beginning to colour and the liver is well sealed.

Stir in the rice and cook for a few minutes more. Add the mushrooms, tomatoes, marjoram (if using), stock and seasonings and bring slowly up to the boil. Mix well, then cover and simmer over a very gentle heat, without stirring, for about 25 minutes, or until the rice is tender and the liquid almost completely absorbed.

Taste and adjust the seasonings, stir in the peas and serve piled on a hot dish. Sprinkle with Parmesan cheese, if liked.

Kidney fritters; Liver risotto; Cidered kidneys

Cidered kidneys

Metric

4 rashers lean back bacon,
derinded and chopped
1 large onion, peeled
and sliced
1 clove garlic, crushed
25 g butter
10 lambs' kidneys,
skinned, halved and cored
A little seasoned flour
450 ml dry cider
Salt and freshly ground
black pepper

To garnish:
1 × 15 ml spoon chopped
chives, optional
2 × 15 ml spoons finely
chopped parsley, optional

Imperial

4 rashers lean back bacon,
derinded and chopped
1 large onion, peeled
and sliced
1 clove garlic, crushed
1 oz butter
10 lambs' kidneys,
skinned, halved and cored
A little seasoned flour
¾ pint dry cider
Salt and freshly ground
black pepper

To garnish:
1 tablespoon chopped
chives, optional
2 tablespoons finely
chopped parsley, optional

Cooking Time: about 25 minutes.

Fry the bacon, onion and garlic in the butter until soft, about 5 minutes. Coat the kidneys in seasoned flour and add to the pan. Fry gently for 7 to 8 minutes, turning several times, until well sealed and almost cooked through. Stir in 1 × 15 ml spoon (1 tablespoon) seasoned flour then gradually add the cider to the pan. Bring to the boil, stirring continuously, then simmer, uncovered, for about 10 minutes, until the kidneys are tender and the sauce has reduced to a syrupy consistency. Taste and adjust the seasonings.

Serve with freshly boiled, buttered spaghetti, and sprinkle liberally with a mixture of the chives and parsley, if liked.

Creamy liver pâté; Liver with lemon glaze; Orchard liver; Liver and bacon pâté

Liver with lemon glaze

Metric

8–12 slices lambs' liver
A little seasoned flour
25 g butter
1 × 15 ml spoon oil

Glaze:
2 × 15 ml spoons oil
3 × 15 ml spoons stock
Finely grated rind of
½ lemon
3 × 15 ml spoons lemon
juice
2 × 15 ml spoons finely
chopped onion
Good pinch of dried
thyme
Salt and freshly ground
black pepper

To garnish:
Lemon slices
Parsley sprigs

Imperial

8–12 slices lambs' liver
A little seasoned flour
1 oz butter
1 tablespoon oil

Glaze:
2 tablespoons oil
3 tablespoons stock
Finely grated rind of
½ lemon
3 tablespoons lemon
juice
2 tablespoons finely
chopped onion
Good pinch of dried
thyme
Salt and freshly ground
black pepper

To garnish:
Lemon slices
Parsley sprigs

Cooking Time: about 20 minutes.

Trim the liver and coat in seasoned flour. Fry in the melted butter and oil for 5 to 8 minutes each side, until well browned and cooked through – but do not overcook or the liver will become hard. Drain on absorbent kitchen paper and keep warm.

Meanwhile, place all the ingredients for the glaze in a small pan and bring to the boil. Simmer gently for 5 to 6 minutes, taste and adjust the seasonings, add to the pan the liver was cooked in and blend with the pan juices. Simmer for 2 to 3 minutes.

Arrange the liver on a flat dish and spoon the glaze over. Garnish with lemon and parsley.

Orchard liver

Metric	Imperial
450 g lambs' liver, sliced	1 lb lambs' liver, sliced
2 × 15 ml spoons seasoned flour	2 tablespoons seasoned flour
25 g butter	1 oz butter
1 × 15 ml spoon oil	1 tablespoon oil
2 medium-sized cooking apples (approx 350 g) peeled, cored and sliced	3 medium-sized cooking apples (approx 12 oz) peeled, cored and sliced
1 × 15 ml spoon finely chopped parsley	1 tablespoon finely chopped parsley
1 × 5 ml spoon finely chopped thyme	1 teaspoon finely chopped thyme
1–2 × 5 ml spoons finely chopped dill or fennel	1–2 teaspoons finely chopped dill or fennel
300 ml stock	½ pint stock
Salt and freshly ground black pepper	Salt and freshly ground black pepper
To garnish:	To garnish:
Sprigs of fresh herbs	Sprigs of fresh herbs

Cooking Time: about 30 minutes.

Coat the liver evenly in the seasoned flour. Melt the butter in a frying pan and add the oil. Fry the liver for 2 to 3 minutes each side until well sealed. Remove from the pan. Add the apples and fry gently for 4 to 5 minutes, taking care not to break up the slices. Sprinkle in the herbs and add the stock. Bring to the boil, season to taste and replace the liver. Cover the pan and simmer gently for 10 to 15 minutes until tender. Taste and adjust the seasonings.
Serve very hot, garnished with sprigs of fresh thyme, fennel and/or dill.

Liver and bacon pâté

Metric	Imperial
275 g streaky bacon rashers, derinded	10 oz streaky bacon rashers, derinded
450 g pigs' liver	1 lb pigs' liver
1 onion, peeled	1 onion, peeled
2 cloves garlic, crushed	2 cloves garlic, crushed
Salt and freshly ground black pepper	Salt and freshly ground black pepper
1 egg, beaten	1 egg, beaten
2 × 15 ml spoons red wine	2 tablespoons red wine
To garnish:	To garnish:
Stuffed olives	Stuffed olives

Cooking Time: 1½ hours.
Oven: 180°C, 350°F, Gas Mark 4.

Finely mince half the bacon with the liver, onion and garlic, twice. Season very well and mix in the egg and wine. Stretch the remaining bacon with the back of a knife and use to line a greased 450 g (1 lb) loaf tin. Spoon in the liver mixture, pressing well down and fold the ends of the bacon over the filling. Stand in a baking tin containing 4 cm (1½ in) water and cook in a moderate oven for 1½ hours. Cool in the tin slightly, then stand a weight on it and chill thoroughly.
Turn out, garnish with stuffed olives and serve in slices with hot toast and butter.
Serves 6.

Creamy liver pâté

Metric	Imperial
50 g butter	2 oz butter
1 small onion, peeled and very finely chopped	1 small onion, peeled and very finely chopped
1–2 cloves garlic, crushed	1–2 cloves garlic, crushed
350 g pigs' liver, chopped	12 oz pigs' liver, chopped
4 × 15 ml spoons white wine	4 tablespoons white wine
Salt and freshly ground black pepper	Salt and freshly ground black pepper
2 × 15 ml spoons brandy or wine	2 tablespoons brandy or wine
2 × 15 ml spoons double cream	2 tablespoons double cream
Melted butter	Melted butter
To garnish:	To garnish:
Cucumber slices	Cucumber slices

Cooking Time: about 30 minutes.

Melt the butter in a pan and fry the onion and garlic until soft. Add the liver and cook gently for 10 minutes, stirring frequently. Add the wine, seasonings, and brandy (if using), cover and simmer for about 20 minutes or until tender. Cool slightly then either blend in a liquidiser until smooth or mince finely twice. Stir in the cream, taste and adjust the seasonings. Spoon into individual dishes or one larger dish and chill until set. Top with a layer of melted butter to cover the pâté and chill again.
Serve garnished with slices of cucumber, with hot fingers of toast.

Liver and bacon marsala

Metric	Imperial
450 g lambs' liver, sliced	1 lb lambs' liver, sliced
Seasoned flour for coating	Seasoned flour for coating
40 g butter	1½ oz butter
8 rashers streaky bacon, derinded and halved	8 rashers streaky bacon, derinded and halved
4 × 15 ml spoons Marsala	4 tablespoons Marsala
150 ml beef stock	¼ pint beef stock
1 × 5 ml spoon lemon juice	1 teaspoon lemon juice
Salt and freshly ground black pepper	Salt and freshly ground black pepper
	To garnish:
To garnish:	Chopped parsley
Chopped parsley	Potato crisps
Potato crisps	

Cooking Time: about 20 minutes.

Trim the liver and coat in seasoned flour. Melt the butter in a frying pan and fry the bacon until lightly coloured. Remove from the pan. Fry the liver until browned on both sides. Add the Marsala, stock and lemon juice and season well. Return the bacon to the pan and simmer gently until the liver is tender and the sauce syrupy, about 15 minutes. Taste and adjust the seasonings, if necessary. Arrange on a serving dish and garnish with parsley and potato crisps.

Soured cream liver

Metric	Imperial
8–12 slices lambs' liver	8–12 slices lambs' liver
A little seasoned flour	A little seasoned flour
25 g butter	1 oz butter
1 large onion, peeled and sliced	1 large onion, peeled and sliced
4–6 tomatoes, peeled and sliced	4–6 tomatoes, peeled and sliced
275 ml stock	Scant ½ pint stock
Salt and freshly ground black pepper	Salt and freshly ground black pepper
Few drops of Worcestershire sauce	Few drops of Worcestershire sauce
2 × 15 ml spoons capers	2 tablespoons capers
150 ml soured cream	¼ pint soured cream

Cooking Time: 25 minutes.

Coat the liver in seasoned flour. Melt the butter in a pan and fry the onion gently until soft and lightly coloured. Add the liver and cook until browned on each side. Stir in the tomatoes, stock, seasoning, Worcestershire sauce and capers and bring slowly to the boil. Cover and simmer gently for about 10 minutes until tender, then continue uncovered for 5 minutes to reduce the sauce a little. Stir in the soured cream and reheat, then taste and adjust the seasonings. Serve with pasta.

Pressed ox tongue

Metric	Imperial
1 ox tongue, fresh or pickled (1¾–2¾ kg)	1 ox tongue, fresh or pickled (4–6 lb)
Bouquet garni	Bouquet garni
1 onion, peeled and sliced	1 onion, peeled and sliced
2 carrots, peeled and sliced	2 carrots, peeled and sliced
Few black peppercorns	Few black peppercorns
To garnish:	To garnish:
Mixed salads	Mixed salads

Cooking Time: 3–6 hours depending on size.

If pickled, soak the tongue in cold water for several hours. Place the tongue in a saucepan with the bouquet garni, onion, carrot and peppercorns and cover with cold water. Bring to the boil, remove the scum, cover and simmer gently for 2½–3 hours if pickled and 4½–6 hours if fresh, until tender. Plunge into cold water when ready and strip off the skin, removing any pieces of bone and gristle.
Put the tongue into a conveniently sized cake tin or basin. (A 2¾ kg (6 lb) tongue fits into an 18 cm (7 in) round cake tin.) Add a little stock, put a plate on top and weight down heavily until cold and set. Turn out and serve with salads.

Note: to serve hot, sprinkle the skinned tongue with toasted breadcrumbs, garnish with wedges of lemon and serve with a parsley sauce.

Liver and bacon marsala; Soured cream liver; Pressed ox tongue; Braised lambs' tongues

Braised lambs' tongues

Metric

4 lambs' tongues
2 onions, peeled and
sliced
1 × 15 ml spoon oil
2 carrots, peeled and
diced
226 g can peeled tomatoes
Salt and freshly ground
black pepper
About 450 ml stock
1 × 15 ml spoon freshly
chopped parsley
1 × 15 ml spoon capers or
chopped gherkins

To garnish:
Bacon rolls

Imperial

4 lambs' tongues
2 onions, peeled and
sliced
1 tablespoon oil
2 carrots, peeled and
diced
8 oz can peeled tomatoes
Salt and freshly ground
black pepper
About ¾ pint stock
1 tablespoon freshly
chopped parsley
1 tablespoon capers or
chopped gherkins

To garnish:
Bacon rolls

Cooking Time: about 1½ hours.
Oven: 180°C, 350°F, Gas Mark 4.

Wash the tongues thoroughly and trim if necessary. Fry the onions in oil until golden brown then transfer to an ovenproof casserole. Lay the tongues on the onion and surround with the carrot and tomatoes. Season well, pour in sufficient stock just to cover and sprinkle with the parsley, and capers or gherkins. Cover and cook in a moderate oven for about 1½ hours, until tender. Taste and adjust the seasonings. The tongues can be removed and skinned, and then reheated again in the sauce before serving, if preferred. Serve garnished with bacon rolls.

Stuffed lambs' hearts

Metric	Imperial
4 lambs' hearts	4 lambs' hearts
1 small onion, peeled and finely chopped	1 small onion, peeled and finely chopped
2 rashers streaky bacon, derinded and chopped	2 rashers streaky bacon, derinded and chopped
2 small sticks celery, scrubbed and finely chopped	2 small sticks celery, scrubbed and finely chopped
25 g butter	1 oz butter
75 g cooked rice	3 oz cooked rice
Salt and freshly ground black pepper	Salt and freshly ground black pepper
Good pinch of ground mace	Good pinch of ground mace
40 g raisins	1½ oz raisins
300 ml stock	½ pint stock
1 × 15 ml spoon vinegar	1 tablespoon vinegar
1 × 15 ml spoon cornflour	1 tablespoon cornflour
To garnish:	To garnish:
Freshly cooked carrots and peas	Freshly cooked carrots and peas

Cooking Time: 2½–3 hours.
Oven: 160°C, 325°F, Gas Mark 3.

Wash the hearts very thoroughly, slit open a little and remove any tubes or gristle. Wash again and dry well. Fry the onion, bacon and celery in the melted butter until lightly browned. Add the rice, seasonings, mace and raisins and mix well. Use to stuff the cavities in the hearts then tie into shape with fine string if necessary. Place the hearts in an ovenproof casserole just large enough to take them. Bring the stock to the boil, add the vinegar, season well and add to the casserole. Cover and cook in a warm oven for 2–2½ hours, until tender.

Strain off the liquor and thicken with cornflour blended in a little cold water. Bring to the boil for 2 minutes, taste and adjust the seasonings.

Arrange the hearts on a serving dish, spoon the sauce over and garnish with carrots and peas.

Seville heart pie

Metric	Imperial
1–1¼ kg ox heart	2–2½ lb ox heart
3 × 15 ml spoons oil	3 tablespoons oil
2 large onions, peeled and sliced	2 large onions, peeled and sliced
3 × 15 ml spoons flour	3 tablespoons flour
450 ml stock	¾ pint stock
Finely grated rind and juice of 1 large orange	Finely grated rind and juice of 1 large orange
Salt and freshly ground black pepper	Salt and freshly ground black pepper
2 × 15 ml spoons port (optional)	2 tablespoons port (optional)
1 orange, peeled and cut into segments	1 orange, peeled and cut into segments
675 g creamed potato	1½ lb creamed potato
To garnish:	To garnish:
Julienne strips of orange (see note)	Julienne strips of orange (see note)

Cooking Time: 3½–4 hours.
Oven: 150°C, 300°F, Gas Mark 2,
   200°C, 400°F, Gas Mark 6.

Cut the heart into narrow strips, removing any tubes and gristle, then wash very thoroughly and dry. Fry in the oil until lightly browned and transfer to an ovenproof casserole. Fry the onion in the same fat until soft, then stir in the flour and cook for 1 minute. Gradually add the stock and bring to the boil for 2 minutes. Stir in the orange rind, juice, seasonings and port (if using). Pour into the casserole, cover and cook in a cool oven for about 3 hours, or until tender, adding a little more stock, if necessary, during the cooking.

Remove the lid, taste and adjust the seasonings and stir in the orange segments. Pipe the potato over the casserole, leaving a gap in the centre. Return to a moderately hot oven for about 30 minutes, until the potato is lightly browned. Serve sprinkled with julienne strips of orange.

Note: to make julienne strips, finely pare the rind from a firm orange, free of white pith, using a potato peeler. Cut into very thin long strips and then simmer gently in boiling water for 10 minutes, or until tender. Drain well.

Seville heart pie; Stuffed lambs' hearts; Hearts victoriana

Hearts victoriana

Metric	Imperial
3 large or 4 small lambs' hearts	*3 large or 4 small lambs' hearts*
25 g butter or margarine	*1 oz butter or margarine*
2 onions, peeled and sliced	*2 onions, peeled and sliced*
2 × 15 ml spoons flour	*2 tablespoons flour*
600 ml stock	*1 pint stock*
2 × 5 ml spoons basil or oregano	*2 teaspoons basil or oregano*
Salt and freshly ground black pepper	*Salt and freshly ground black pepper*
50 g sultanas or raisins	*2 oz sultanas or raisins*
1 large cooking apple, peeled, cored and sliced	*1 large cooking apple, peeled, cored and sliced*
Apple slices to garnish (optional)	*Apple slices to garnish (optional)*

Cooking Time: 2¼ hours.
Oven: 160°C, 325°F, Gas Mark 3.

Wash the hearts thoroughly and cut into 1 cm (½ in) slices, discarding any gristle and tubes. Fry the heart in melted butter or margarine until well browned and then transfer to an ovenproof casserole. Fry the onions in the same fat until soft then stir in the flour and cook for 1 minute. Gradually add the stock and bring to the boil. Add the herbs, seasonings, and sultanas or raisins, and pour over the hearts. Cover tightly and cook in a warm oven for 1½ hours.

Skim off any fat, taste and adjust the seasonings and add the apple. Continue to cook for a further 30 minutes or until tender.

Garnish with apple slices dipped in lemon juice, if liked.

Shooter's roll

Metric	Imperial
450 g pork sausagemeat, without herbs	1 lb pork sausagemeat, without herbs
100 g lean bacon rashers, derinded and chopped	4 oz lean bacon rashers, derinded and chopped
1 small onion, peeled and finely chopped	1 small onion, peeled and finely chopped
1 × 5 ml spoon dried sage	1 teaspoon dried sage
100 g mushrooms, cleaned, trimmed and finely chopped	4 oz mushrooms, cleaned, trimmed and finely chopped
Salt and freshly ground black pepper	Salt and freshly ground black pepper
350 g frozen puff pastry, thawed	12 oz frozen puff pastry, thawed
Beaten egg to glaze	Beaten egg to glaze
To garnish:	To garnish:
Salads	Salads

Cooking Time: about 50 minutes.
Oven: 230°C, 450°F, Gas Mark 8,
190°C, 375°F, Gas Mark 5.

Combine the sausagemeat, bacon, onion, sage, mushrooms and seasonings to taste. Roll out the pastry thinly on a lightly floured surface and trim to a rectangle approx 30 × 25 cm (12 × 10 in). Form the sausagemeat mixture into a brick shape down the centre of the pastry. Fold over the sides and ends of pastry, damping with water, to enclose the filling completely. Place on a lightly greased or non-stick baking sheet with the pastry joins underneath.

Decorate the roll with the pastry trimmings and brush all over with beaten egg. Make two cuts in the top and bake in a very hot oven for 15 minutes. Reduce oven temperature to moderately hot and continue for a further 35 to 40 minutes. Cover the top with foil if over browning.

Remove carefully from the baking sheet and cool. Chill thoroughly before serving, sliced, with salads.

Chipolata cheese pie

Metric	Imperial
200 g plain flour	8 oz plain flour
Salt and freshly ground black pepper	Salt and freshly ground black pepper
50 g margarine	2 oz margarine
50 g lard or white fat	2 oz lard or white fat
Water to mix	Water to mix
225 g chipolata sausages	8 oz chipolata sausages
2 × 5 ml spoons dripping	2 teaspoons dripping
225 g tomatoes, peeled and sliced	8 oz tomatoes, peeled and sliced
1 large egg	1 large egg
150 ml milk	¼ pint milk
Pinch of garlic powder	Pinch of garlic powder
50 g Cheddar cheese, grated	2 oz Cheddar cheese, grated

Cooking Time: about 1 hour.
Oven: 220°C, 425°F, Gas Mark 7
180°C, 350°F, Gas Mark 4.

Sieve the flour with a pinch of salt into a bowl, add fats and rub in until the mixture resembles fine breadcrumbs. Add sufficient cold water to mix to a pliable dough. Brown the chipolatas lightly in melted dripping, then drain well. Roll out two-thirds of the pastry and use to line a 20 cm (8 in) flan tin or ring. Lay half the tomatoes in the base, cover with the chipolatas and fill in the gaps with the remaining tomatoes. Beat the egg with the milk, seasonings and garlic and pour into the pastry case. Sprinkle with the cheese.

Roll out the remaining pastry, cut into narrow strips and arrange in a lattice pattern over the filling. Cook in a hot oven for 15 minutes, then reduce oven temperature to moderate and continue for 30 to 40 minutes until the filling is golden brown and firm to the touch. Serve hot or cold.

Sausage and bacon piperade

Metric	Imperial
350 g pork, or pork and beef, chipolatas	12 oz pork, or pork and beef, chipolatas
12 long rashers streaky bacon, derinded	12 long rashers streaky bacon, derinded
1 large onion, peeled and thinly sliced	1 large onion, peeled and thinly sliced
2–3 cloves garlic, crushed	2–3 cloves garlic, crushed
50 g butter	2 oz butter
2 × 184 g cans pimientos, drained	2 × 6½ oz cans pimientos, drained
450 g tomatoes, peeled and quartered	1 lb tomatoes, peeled and quartered
Salt and freshly ground black pepper	Salt and freshly ground black pepper

Cooking Time: about 20 minutes.

Prick the chipolatas and wind a rasher of bacon around each one; secure with wooden cocktail sticks if necessary. Either grill or fry, until well browned and cooked through, and keep warm.

Meanwhile, fry the onion and garlic gently in butter until soft, but not brown. Cut the pimientos into thin strips, add to the pan with the tomatoes and cook gently for 7 to 8 minutes, until soft. Season well to taste and turn out on to a warm dish.

Drain the chipolatas on absorbent paper then place on the piperade. Garnish with parsley sprigs, and wedges of hard-boiled egg, if liked.

Chipolata cheese pie; Shooter's roll; Sausage and bacon piperade

Oatmeal sausages with hollandaise sauce

Metric	Imperial
450 g pork sausages with herbs	1 lb pork sausages with herbs
1 egg, beaten	1 egg, beaten
50 g rolled oats	2 oz rolled oats
450 g cooked, chopped spinach	1 lb cooked, chopped spinach
25 g butter	1 oz butter
Salt and freshly ground black pepper	Salt and freshly ground black pepper
A little ground nutmeg	A little ground nutmeg
Sauce:	Sauce:
4 × 15 ml spoons wine vinegar	4 tablespoons wine vinegar
2 × 15 ml spoons water	2 tablespoons water
6 peppercorns, crushed	6 peppercorns, crushed
4 egg yolks	4 egg yolks
100–175 g softened butter	4–6 oz softened butter
A little lemon juice	A little lemon juice
To garnish:	To garnish:
Tomato	Tomato

Cooking Time: about 40 minutes.
Oven: 220°C, 425°F, Gas Mark 7.

Prick the sausages then dip in beaten egg. Coat thoroughly in the oats and place in a greased ovenproof dish. Cook, uncovered, in a hot oven for 35 to 40 minutes, until well browned, crisp and cooked through.

Meanwhile, heat the spinach in melted butter and season to taste with salt, pepper and nutmeg. Turn into a serving dish and keep warm.

To make the sauce, put the vinegar, water and peppercorns in a small pan and bring to the boil. Boil until reduced by half then strain into a basin. Place over a saucepan of gently simmering water. Beat in the egg yolks and cook very gently until the sauce thickens, stirring continuously. Beat in the butter, a little at a time until the sauce has a thin coating consistency. Season to taste, sharpen with a little lemon juice.

Drain the sausages and arrange on the spinach. Garnish with tomato. Serve with the warm sauce.

Sausage nuggets

Metric	Imperial
3 hard-boiled eggs, chopped	3 hard-boiled eggs, chopped
75 g English Mature Cheddar cheese, grated	3 oz English Mature Cheddar cheese, grated
2 × 15 ml spoons tomato ketchup	2 tablespoons tomato ketchup
Salt and freshly ground black pepper	Salt and freshly ground black pepper
450 g fresh sausagemeat	1 lb fresh sausagemeat
2 × 15 ml spoons very finely chopped onion	2 tablespoons very finely chopped onion
Flour for coating	Flour for coating
1 egg, beaten	1 egg, beaten
Golden crumbs for coating	Golden crumbs for coating
Deep fat for frying	Deep fat for frying
To garnish:	To garnish:
Lettuce leaves	Lettuce leaves
Carrot sticks	Carrot sticks

Cooking Time: 15 minutes.

Mix together the chopped eggs, grated cheese, ketchup, and seasonings to taste. Divide into four equal portions and form into balls. Combine the sausagemeat with the onion and divide into four. Mould each piece of sausagemeat around a cheese and egg ball to give an egg shape. Roll first in flour, then dip in beaten egg and finally coat in breadcrumbs; chill until required.

Heat the deep fat until it is hot enough to brown a cube of bread in 20 to 30 seconds – 180–190°C/350–375°F. Fry the nuggets for about 15 minutes, or until crisp, golden brown and cooked through. Drain on absorbent kitchen paper and serve hot or cold with a garnish of lettuce and carrot sticks.

Oatmeal sausages; Sausage nuggets; Sausage and bacon casserole

Sausage and bacon casserole

Metric

450 g pork or beef
sausages
1 × 15 ml spoon dripping
12 rashers streaky bacon,
derinded and rolled
1 large onion, peeled and
sliced
2 large carrots, peeled
and sliced
100 g button mushrooms,
cleaned, trimmed and
halved
300 ml stock
4–6 × 15 ml spoons red
wine
1 × 5 ml spoon dried
thyme
Salt and freshly ground
black pepper
½ teaspoon
Worcestershire sauce
4 tomatoes, peeled and
halved

Imperial

1 lb pork or beef
sausages
1 tablespoon dripping
12 rashers streaky bacon,
derinded and rolled
1 large onion, peeled and
sliced
2 large carrots, peeled
and sliced
4 oz button mushrooms,
cleaned, trimmed and
halved
½ pint stock
4–6 tablespoons red wine
1 teaspoon dried thyme
Salt and freshly ground
black pepper
½ teaspoon Worcestershire
sauce
4 tomatoes, peeled and
halved

Cooking Time: 1¼ hours.
Oven: 180°C, 350°F, Gas Mark 4.

Brown the sausages in the melted dripping then transfer to an ovenproof casserole. Fry the bacon in the same fat until lightly browned and add to the casserole. Add the onion, carrots and mushrooms to the pan and cook gently for 5 minutes. Stir in the stock, wine, thyme, seasonings and Worcestershire sauce and bring to the boil. Pour into the casserole, cover and cook in a moderate oven for 40 minutes. Remove any fat from the surface, taste and adjust the seasonings and add the tomatoes. Continue cooking for 20 minutes.

Note: this dish can be thickened with a little cornflour if preferred.

Hot sausage and potato salad

Metric

450–675 g new potatoes, scraped
Salt and freshly ground black pepper
450 g fresh chipolatas
1 bunch spring onions, cleaned and trimmed
340 g can pineapple cubes or rings, diced
1 × 15 ml spoon finely chopped parsley
4–6 gherkins, sliced

Dressing:
3 × 15 ml spoons oil
1 × 15 ml spoon wine vinegar
Large pinch dry mustard
1 clove garlic, crushed

To garnish:
Lettuce or curly endive

Imperial

1–1½ lb new potatoes, scraped
Salt and freshly ground black pepper
1 lb fresh chipolatas
1 bunch spring onions, cleaned and trimmed
12 oz can pineapple cubes or rings, diced
1 tablespoon finely chopped parsley
4–6 gherkins, sliced

Dressing:
3 tablespoons oil
1 tablespoon wine vinegar
Large pinch dry mustard
1 clove garlic, crushed

To garnish:
Lettuce or curly endive

Cooking Time: about 40 minutes.

Boil the potatoes in salted water until just tender. Drain, cut into quarters and keep warm. Grill or fry the chipolatas until cooked through and well browned, then drain and cut each one into three slanting slices; keep warm. Slice half the onions and place in a bowl with the drained pineapple, parsley and gherkins. Mix the dressing ingredients, 1 × 15 ml spoon (1 tablespoon) pineapple juice and plenty of seasonings together and add to the pineapple mixture with the hot potatoes and chipolatas.

Toss thoroughly and serve at once garnished with the remaining spring onions and with lettuce or endive.

Sausage and salami tattie ash

Metric

450 g fresh sausages
1 × 15 ml spoon dripping
1 large onion, peeled and sliced
450 g small new potatoes, scraped or scrubbed
2 carrots, peeled and cut into sticks
1 large leek, trimmed, sliced and washed
100 g salami, diced
Salt and freshly ground black pepper
1 × 5 ml spoon Worcestershire sauce
400 ml stock

To garnish:
Salami slices, optional
Chopped parsley, optional

Imperial

1 lb fresh sausages
1 tablespoon dripping
1 large onion, peeled and sliced
1 lb small new potatoes, scraped or scrubbed
2 carrots, peeled and cut into sticks
1 large leek, trimmed, sliced and washed
4 oz salami, diced
Salt and freshly ground black pepper
1 teaspoon Worcestershire sauce
Scant ¾ pint stock

To garnish:
Salami slices, optional
Chopped parsley, optional

Cooking Time: about 1 hour.
Oven: 180°C, 350°F, Gas Mark 4.

Fry the sausages quickly in melted dripping until well browned all over; drain and cut each one in half. Fry the onion in the same fat until lightly browned, then drain well. Place the sausages, onion, potatoes (which can be left in their skins, if preferred), carrots, leek, salami and seasonings in an ovenproof casserole. Add the Worcestershire sauce to the stock and pour into the casserole. Cover and cook in a moderate oven for about 1 hour or until tender.

Taste and adjust the seasonings and serve garnished with slices of salami and chopped parsley, if liked.

Note: cocktail sausages or chipolatas can be used in place of ordinary sausages.

Sausage and salami tattie ash; Hot sausage and potato salad; Sausagemeat flan

Sausagemeat flan

Metric

450 g fresh sausagemeat
1 small onion, peeled
and finely chopped
50 g fresh breadcrumbs
Salt and freshly ground
black pepper
1 egg, beaten
3 leeks, trimmed, thickly
sliced and washed
25 g butter
25 g flour
250 ml milk
½ teaspoon mustard
75 g English Mature
Cheddar cheese, grated

Imperial

1 lb fresh sausagemeat
1 small onion, peeled
and finely chopped
2 oz fresh breadcrumbs
Salt and freshly ground
black pepper
1 egg, beaten
3 leeks, trimmed, thickly
sliced and washed
1 oz butter
1 oz flour
Scant ½ pint milk
½ teaspoon mustard
3 oz English Mature
Cheddar cheese, grated

Cooking Time: about 40 minutes.
Oven: 200°C, 400°F, Gas Mark 6.

Mix the sausagemeat with the onion, breadcrumbs, seasonings and beaten egg. Use to line a lightly greased 18 cm (7 in) flan dish. Cook in a moderately hot oven for 25 to 30 minutes until well browned and cooked through. Meanwhile, cook the leeks in salted water until tender and then drain very thoroughly. Melt the butter in a pan, stir in the flour and cook for 1 minute, then gradually add the milk and bring to the boil for 2 minutes. Season to taste, then stir in the mustard and most of the cheese until melted. Add the leeks and pour into the flan. Sprinkle with the remaining cheese and return to the oven or place under a moderate grill until the cheese is lightly browned, about 10 minutes. Serve hot.

Sizzling hot food, cooked and eaten in the open air, has a very special flavour. The kind of barbecue equipment you use doesn't matter, so long as it does its job of producing well cooked, flavoursome food. Always light your barbecue in good time, because it takes time to heat and you should not begin to cook until the flames have died down and the charcoal is glowing. Flames will only char the food and not give enough heat to cook it right through.

Remember that food (whether raw or part-cooked), taken straight from the fridge, will need longer cooking on the barbecue than food at room temperature.

For fine quality steaks and chops, the charcoal cooking gives a perfect flavour which need not be added to by marinade or sauce. But many other meats will become more tender and gain in flavour after 2–24 hours in a marinade. If you do not use a marinade, brush the meat with melted butter or oil before and during cooking.

Salt added to meat before barbecue-cooking will cause the juices to splutter on to the fire, so add seasonings to the cooked foods. Turn the meat frequently during cooking.

Meats suitable for the barbecue:
LAMB – cutlets, chops, kidneys, liver, strips of leg of lamb, pieces of breast of lamb, fillet.
PORK – chops, spare ribs, strips of lean belly, liver, kidneys, tenderloin or fillet. Pork should be thoroughly cooked.
BEEF – all types of steak.
You can also barbecue-cook: all types of sausage, bacon chops or thick rashers of bacon, meatballs, hamburgers and kebabs.

Important: All the recipes which follow are designed to be cooked on a barbecue, but instructions are given for cooking under a conventional grill, in case you have no barbecue. On a barbecue, the cooking timings may vary according to its heat.
A word of warning: don't use expensive kebab skewers with fancy handles on a barbecue – they can burn very easily.

Lemon barbecue sauce

Metric	Imperial
40 g butter	*1½ oz butter*
1 clove garlic, crushed	*1 clove garlic, crushed*
1 small onion, peeled and thinly sliced	*1 small onion, peeled and thinly sliced*
2 × 5 ml spoons flour	*2 teaspoons flour*
200 ml dry white wine	*7 fl oz dry white wine*
Grated rind of 1 lemon	*Grated rind of 1 lemon*
Juice of 2 lemons	*Juice of 2 lemons*
1 lemon, thinly sliced	*1 lemon, thinly sliced*
Few drops Tabasco sauce	*Few drops Tabasco sauce*
Salt and freshly ground black pepper	*Salt and freshly ground black pepper*
Pinch of chilli powder	*Pinch of chilli powder*
Sugar to taste	*Sugar to taste*
Chopped parsley (optional)	*Chopped parsley (optional)*

Cooking Time: 12 minutes.

Melt the butter and fry the garlic and onion gently until soft. Stir in the flour followed by the wine, lemon rind and juice and bring to the boil, stirring continuously. Add the sliced lemon, Tabasco, seasonings, chilli powder and sugar to taste and simmer for 5 minutes. Taste and adjust the seasonings and serve hot with 1 × 15 ml spoon (1 tablespoon) freshly chopped parsley added, if liked. Serve with any meats.
Note: dry cider or half wine and half stock may be used in place of all wine.

Marinade for meat

Metric	Imperial
Strip of finely pared orange rind	*Strip of finely pared orange rind*
2 × 15 ml spoons wine vinegar	*2 tablespoons wine vinegar*
150 ml red wine or sherry	*¼ pint red wine or sherry*
Freshly ground black pepper	*Freshly ground black pepper*
1 × 5 ml spoon coarse salt	*1 teaspoon coarse salt*
2 × 5 ml spoons soft brown sugar	*2 teaspoons soft brown sugar*
Few sprigs fresh thyme (or rosemary for lamb)	*Few sprigs fresh thyme (or rosemary for lamb)*
Few drops Worcestershire sauce	*Few drops Worcestershire sauce*

Put all the ingredients together in a bowl and mix well. Add the meat and sufficient cold water barely to cover. Cover the bowl and put in the refrigerator or cold place for up to 24 hours, turning the meat occasionally. Before cooking, drain the meat well and brush with oil or melted butter. Heat the marinade gently and bring up to the boil. Simmer for 5 minutes, thicken with a little cornflour, if liked, and serve with the cooked meats.
Note: for larger quantities of meat, double the recipe.

Barbecuing meats; Lemon barbecue sauce; Marinade for meat

Tomato barbecue sauce

Metric

1 × 15 ml spoon vinegar
1½ × 15 ml spoons brown sugar
1½ × 5 ml spoons mustard
¼ teaspoon freshly ground black pepper
¾ teaspoon salt
¾ × 5 ml spoon salt
Good pinch cayenne
Good pinch grated lemon rind
1 × 5 ml spoon lemon juice
1 small onion, peeled and finely chopped
25 g butter
4 × 15 ml spoons tomato ketchup
1 × 15 ml spoon Worcestershire sauce
8 stuffed olives, chopped

Imperial

1 tablespoon vinegar
1½ tablespoons brown sugar
1½ teaspoons mustard
¼ teaspoon freshly ground black pepper
¾ teaspoon salt
Good pinch cayenne
Good pinch grated lemon rind
1 teaspoon lemon juice
1 small onion, peeled and finely chopped
1 oz butter
4 tablespoons tomato ketchup
1 tablespoon Worcestershire sauce
8 stuffed olives, chopped

Cooking Time: 15–20 minutes.

Place all the ingredients, except the olives, with 4 × 15 ml spoons (4 tablespoons) water, in a small saucepan and bring slowly to the boil. Cover and simmer gently for about 15 minutes, stirring from time to time, then stir in the olives. Serve hot or cold in a bowl to eat with any barbecued meats. This sauce will keep for several days in a covered container in the refrigerator and the quantities can be doubled up to serve larger numbers.

Shish kebabs

Metric

1¼ kg piece top of leg of lamb
4 × 15 ml spoons oil
2 × 15 ml spoons wine vinegar
2 × 15 ml spoons lemon juice
1 clove garlic, crushed
Salt and freshly ground black pepper
1 small onion, peeled and finely chopped
8 bay leaves
8 thick slices of raw onion, blanched

To garnish:
Parsley sprigs
Lemon wedges

Imperial

2½ lb piece top of leg of lamb
4 tablespoons oil
2 tablespoons wine vinegar
2 tablespoons lemon juice
1 clove garlic, crushed
Salt and freshly ground black pepper
1 small onion, peeled and finely chopped
8 bay leaves
8 thick slices of raw onion, blanched

To garnish:
Parsley sprigs
Lemon wedges

Cooking Time: 2 hours for marinading, plus about 20 minutes.

Trim the lamb and cut into 2·5 cm (1 in) cubes. Place the oil in a bowl with the vinegar, lemon juice, garlic, seasonings and chopped onion. Add the meat and leave in a cool place to marinade for at least 2 hours, turning several times.
Drain the cubes of meat and thread on to 4 long skewers, alternating with the bay leaves and slices of onion. Cook under a moderately hot grill for about 10 minutes each side, until browned and cooked through; or cook over a charcoal barbecue until tender. Garnish with lemon wedges and parsley and serve with a plain or savoury rice.

Shish kebabs; Tomato barbecue sauce; Sausage and bacon skewers

Sausage and bacon skewers

Metric

300–350 g slice gammon (2 cm thick)
425 g can peach halves
225 g chipolatas, halved
8 fresh bay leaves
8 button onions, peeled and blanched

Coleslaw:
350 g finely shredded white cabbage
2 large carrots, peeled and coarsely grated
1 × 15 ml spoon finely chopped parsley
25 g shelled walnuts, roughly chopped
3–4 × 15 ml spoons French dressing

Imperial

10–12 oz slice gammon (¾ inch thick)
15 oz can peach halves
8 oz chipolatas, halved
8 fresh bay leaves
8 button onions, peeled and blanched

Coleslaw:
12 oz finely shredded white cabbage
2 large carrots, peeled and coarsely grated
1 tablespoon finely chopped parsley
1 oz shelled walnuts, roughly chopped
3–4 tablespoons French dressing

Cooking Time: about 15 minutes.

Cut the gammon into 2 cm (¾ in) cubes after discarding the rind. Drain the peaches and cut each piece in half. Arrange the gammon, pieces of peach, chipolatas, bay leaves and onions on 4 long skewers. Cook under a moderate grill for about 15 minutes, turning several times and brushing regularly with peach juice, until the chipolatas and bacon are cooked through. Serve on a bed of coleslaw. For the coleslaw, combine the cabbage, carrots, parsley, walnuts and sufficient French dressing to coat evenly.

Pork and lemon brochettes

Metric

550–675 g pork fillet
2 onions, peeled, thickly
sliced and blanched
2 × 15 ml spoons lemon
juice
A little oil

Sauce:
200 ml stock
1 × 15 ml spoon soy sauce
Good dash of
Worcestershire sauce
1 × 5 ml spoon lemon
juice
Salt and freshly ground
black pepper
1 × 5 ml spoon cornflour
2 tomatoes, peeled,
deseeded and chopped

To garnish:
Lemon wedges
Watercress sprigs

Imperial

1¼–1½ lb pork fillet
2 onions, peeled, thickly
sliced and blanched
2 tablespoons lemon juice
A little oil

Sauce:
7 fl oz stock
1 tablespoon soy sauce
Good dash of
Worcestershire sauce
1 teaspoon lemon juice
Salt and freshly ground
black pepper
1 teaspoon cornflour
2 tomatoes, peeled,
deseeded and chopped

To garnish:
Lemon wedges
Watercress sprigs

Cooking Time: about 25 minutes.

Trim the pork and cut into thin strips about 4 cm (1½ in) long by 1·5 cm (½ in) thick. Arrange on 4 long skewers, pushing the meat fairly tightly together and interspersing with slices of onion. Brush the pork first with lemon juice and then with oil. Place on a grill rack and cook under a moderate heat until the meat is well browned and cooked through, about 8 to 10 minutes each side. Brush with the oil several times during cooking.

Meanwhile, to make the sauce, place the stock, soy sauce, Worcestershire sauce, lemon juice and seasonings in a pan and bring to the boil. Thicken with the cornflour blended in a little cold water and add the tomato. Simmer for 5 minutes, then serve with the kebabs. Garnish with lemon and sprigs of watercress.

Marinaded beef kebabs

Metric

150 ml natural yogurt
150 ml tomato juice
2 × 5 ml spoons
Worcestershire sauce
Pinch of cayenne
1 × 5 ml spoon dried sage
½ teaspoon marjoram
1 × 15 ml spoon finely
chopped onion
Salt and freshly ground
black pepper
450 g rump steak
8 mushrooms, cleaned
4 tomatoes, halved
1 green pepper, washed,
deseeded and cut into 8

Imperial

5 fl oz natural yogurt
¼ pint tomato juice
2 teaspoons
Worcestershire sauce
Pinch of cayenne
1 teaspoon dried sage
½ teaspoon marjoram
1 tablespoon finely
chopped onion
Salt and freshly ground
black pepper
1 lb rump steak
8 mushrooms, cleaned
4 tomatoes, halved
1 green pepper, washed,
deseeded and cut into 8

Cooking Time: about 5 hours for marinading, plus 15–20 minutes.

Mix together the yogurt, tomato juice, Worcestershire sauce, cayenne, herbs, onion and seasonings. Trim the steak and cut into 2·5 cm (1 in) cubes. Place in the marinade and leave for 4 to 5 hours, turning occasionally. Drain the meat and thread on to 4 long skewers, alternating with the mushrooms, tomatoes and pepper. Cook under a hot grill, brushing with the marinade frequently and turning the meat once or twice until well browned but not overcooked.

Heat the marinade gently, without boiling, taste and adjust the seasonings and serve with the kebabs and saffron rice.
Note: to make saffron rice, add a few grains of saffron or a little powdered turmeric to the boiling salted water before adding the rice.

Marinaded beef kebabs; Pork and lemon brochettes; Liver and bacon kebabs

Liver and bacon kebabs

Metric

450 g lambs' liver in a
piece
4 × 15 ml spoons oil
2 × 15 ml spoons lemon
juice
Salt and freshly ground
black pepper
12 rashers streaky bacon,
derinded and rolled
8 large button mushrooms,
cleaned and trimmed
8 fresh bay leaves
4 large tomatoes, halved
Saffron rice
150 ml stock

Imperial

1 lb lambs' liver in a
piece
4 tablespoons oil
2 tablespoons lemon juice
Salt and freshly ground
black pepper
12 rashers streaky bacon,
derinded and rolled
8 large button mushrooms,
cleaned and trimmed
8 fresh bay leaves
4 large tomatoes, halved
Saffron rice
¼ pint stock

Cooking Time: about 2 hours for marinading, plus about 15 minutes.

Cut the liver into 2 cm/¾ inch cubes and place in a bowl with the oil, lemon juice and seasonings and marinade for 1–2 hours.

Drain the liver well and arrange on four long skewers with the bacon rolls, mushrooms and bay leaves. Place on the grill rack and cook under a moderate grill for about 5 minutes each side, brushing once or twice with the marinade, until browned. Grill the tomatoes alongside the kebabs. Place on a bed of saffron rice with the tomatoes to garnish. Keep warm. Add the stock to the pan juices and bring to the boil for 1 to 2 minutes. Taste and adjust the seasonings and pour over the kebabs.

Note: to make saffron rice, add a few grains of saffron or a little powdered turmeric to the boiling salted water before adding the rice.

Veal bigarade

Metric

4 escalopes of veal, beaten flat
Salt and freshly ground black pepper
40 g butter
2 × 15 ml spoons wine vinegar
2 × 15 ml spoons caster sugar
Finely grated rind of 1 orange
Juice of 3 large oranges
2 × 15 ml spoons lemon juice
300 ml white stock
1 × 15 ml spoon cornflour (optional)
2 × 15 ml spoons brandy

To garnish:
1 orange, thinly sliced
Watercress sprigs

Imperial

4 escalopes of veal, beaten flat
Salt and freshly ground black pepper
1½ oz butter
2 tablespoons wine vinegar
2 tablespoons caster sugar
Finely grated rind of 1 orange
Juice of 3 large oranges
2 tablespoons lemon juice
½ pint white stock
1 tablespoon cornflour (optional)
2 tablespoons brandy

To garnish:
1 orange, thinly sliced
Watercress sprigs

Cooking Time: about 30 minutes.

Trim the veal and season lightly with salt and pepper. Melt the butter in a large frying pan and cook the escalopes gently for 3 to 4 minutes on each side. Keep warm. Meanwhile heat the vinegar and sugar together in a small pan, without stirring, until caramel coloured. Add the orange rind, fruit juices and stock and bring to the boil. Simmer gently, uncovered, for 5 minutes, stirring occasionally. Blend the cornflour (if using) in a little cold water and add to the sauce; bring to the boil for 2 minutes. Add to the escalopes in the pan and cook gently for 5 minutes, spooning the sauce over the meat continuously. Warm the brandy, set alight and add to the pan. Stir until evenly mixed, taste and adjust seasonings.
Serve immediately, garnished with twists of orange and watercress.

Veal bigarade

Colonial goose

Metric

2 kg leg of lamb, boned
25 g butter
1 small onion, peeled
and chopped
100 g prunes, soaked
1 eating apple, peeled
cored and chopped
75 g fresh breadcrumbs
Salt and freshly ground
black pepper
1 × 5 ml spoon fresh or
dried rosemary, finely
chopped
1 egg, beaten
150 ml dry white wine
A little melted butter
2 × 15 ml spoons flour
300 ml stock

To garnish:
Cooked courgettes, sliced
Cooked whole prunes
Fresh rosemary
(optional)

Imperial

4½ lb leg of lamb, boned
1 oz butter
1 small onion, peeled
and chopped
4 oz prunes, soaked
1 eating apple, peeled,
cored and chopped
3 oz fresh breadcrumbs
Salt and freshly ground
black pepper
1 teaspoon fresh or dried
rosemary, finely chopped
1 egg, beaten
¼ pint dry white wine
A little melted butter
2 tablespoons flour
½ pint stock

To garnish:
Cooked courgettes, sliced
Cooked whole prunes
Fresh rosemary
(optional)

Cooking Time: about 4–6 hours for marinading, plus 2½–3 hours. Oven: 180°C, 350°F, Gas Mark 4.

Ask the butcher to bone out the leg of lamb – this may have to be ordered in advance. Melt the butter and fry the onion until soft. Chop and stone the prunes and add to the onion with the apple, breadcrumbs, seasonings and rosemary. Bind together with the egg and use to stuff the bone cavity. Sew the joint back into shape with a trussing needle and fine string – but not too tightly or the skin will split during cooking. Place in a polythene bag, lining a bowl, add the wine and marinade for 4–6 hours, turning occasionally. Remove the joint, weigh and place in a roasting tin. Brush with melted butter and cook in a moderate oven, allowing 25 minutes per 450 g (1 lb), plus 30 minutes over. Baste occasionally and cover with foil when sufficiently browned. Remove the string from the joint, place joint on a serving dish and keep warm. Pour off the fat from the roasting tin and stir the flour into the pan juices. Cook for a few minutes then stir in the wine marinade and stock. Bring to the boil and simmer for 2 minutes. Taste and adjust the seasonings and strain into a sauce boat. Garnish the joint with slices of courgette, whole prunes, and sprigs of rosemary if available.

Colonial goose

Gaelic steaks

Metric	Imperial
50 g butter	2 oz butter
1 × 15 ml spoon oil	1 tablespoon oil
1 large onion, peeled and finely chopped	1 large onion, peeled and finely chopped
1 clove garlic, crushed (optional)	1 clove garlic, crushed (optional)
Salt and freshly ground black pepper	Salt and freshly ground black pepper
4 fresh home-produced sirloin steaks	4 fresh home-produced sirloin steaks
3–4 × 15 ml spoons whisky	3–4 tablespoons whisky
2 × 15 ml spoons finely chopped parsley	2 tablespoons finely chopped parsley
1 × 5 ml spoon lemon juice	1 teaspoon lemon juice

Cooking Time: about 20 minutes.

Melt the butter and oil together in a large heavy frying pan. Add the onion and garlic (if using) and sauté gently for about 5 minutes without colouring. Season the steaks lightly with salt and generously with pepper. Add to the pan and fry quickly for 2 to 4 minutes on each side (depending on how rare they are required to be). Warm the whisky, add to the pan and flambé. Stir in the parsley and lemon juice. Turn the steaks over and cook gently for $\frac{1}{2}$ to 1 minute. Taste and adjust the seasonings, if necessary. Serve immediately.

Steak parcels; Beef stroganoff

Gaelic steaks

Beef stroganoff

Metric	Imperial
550–675 g rump or fillet steak	1¼–1½ lb rump or fillet steak
50 g butter	2 oz butter
1 × 5 ml spoon oil	1 teaspoon oil
2 large onions, peeled and thinly sliced	2 large onions, peeled and thinly sliced
225 g button mushrooms, cleaned, trimmed and sliced	8 oz button mushrooms, cleaned, trimmed and sliced
Salt and freshly ground black pepper	Salt and freshly ground black pepper
200–300 ml soured cream	7 fl oz–½ pint soured cream

To garnish:
Chopped chives or parsley

To garnish:
Chopped chives or parsley

Cooking Time: about 15 minutes.

Trim the steak and cut into narrow strips about 5 cm × 6 mm (2 in × ¼ in). Melt 25 g (1 oz) butter in a pan, add the oil and fry the onion until soft and just beginning to colour. Add the mushrooms and continue for 3 to 4 minutes. Remove from the pan and keep warm. Add the remaining butter to the pan and, when hot, fry the steak quickly for 4 to 5 minutes, stirring frequently. Return the onions and mushrooms to the pan and season. Stir in the soured cream and heat through quickly for 2 minutes Taste and adjust the seasonings and serve immediately, sprinkled with chives or parsley.

Steak parcels

Metric	Imperial
40 g butter	1½ oz butter
100 g mushrooms, cleaned, trimmed and chopped	4 oz mushrooms, cleaned, trimmed and chopped
1 clove garlic, crushed	1 clove garlic, crushed
1 × 5 ml spoon French mustard	1 teaspoon French mustard
1 × 15 ml spoon finely chopped parsley	1 tablespoon finely chopped parsley
Salt and freshly ground black pepper	Salt and freshly ground black pepper
4 minute steaks (150–175 g each)	4 minute steaks (5–6 oz each)
450 g puff pastry	1 lb puff pastry
Beaten egg to glaze	Beaten egg to glaze
Deep fat for frying	Deep fat for frying

Cooking Time: about 15 minutes.

Melt half the butter in a pan and fry the mushrooms and garlic until soft. Stir in the mustard and parsley, season well and leave to cool. Season the steaks lightly, then fry quickly in the remaining butter for 1–1½ minutes each side. Remove from pan, spread with mushroom mixture. Cool. Roll out the pastry thinly and cut out circles large enough to enclose each steak. Position steaks on the pastry, brush the edges with beaten egg and press together to enclose the steaks completely. Make sure the pastry is securely pinched together. Turn the parcels over and brush with egg. Decorate with the pastry trimmings and brush again with egg. Heat the fat to about 180°C/350°F, or until a cube of bread browns in it in 20 seconds, and carefully lower the parcels into the fat, two at a time. Fry for about 5 minutes, turning over once, until golden brown. Drain on absorbent paper. Garnish with watercress, chicory, carrot sticks, if liked.

Veal Jessica

Metric	Imperial
4 veal cutlets	4 veal cutlets
Salt and freshly ground black pepper	Salt and freshly ground black pepper
1 clove garlic, crushed	1 clove garlic, crushed
40 g butter	1½ oz butter
1 onion, peeled and thinly sliced	1 onion, peeled and thinly sliced
396 g can peeled tomatoes	14 oz can peeled tomatoes
2 × 15 ml spoons red wine	2 tablespoons red wine
100 g mozarella cheese, sliced	4 oz mozarella cheese, sliced
To garnish:	To garnish:
Fresh herbs	Fresh herbs

Cooking Time: about 1 hour.
Oven: 180°C, 350°F, Gas Mark 4.

Trim the cutlets, season with salt and pepper and rub with the garlic. Fry in the melted butter until well browned on both sides. Transfer to a shallow ovenproof casserole. Fry the onion in the same fat until soft and arrange over the veal. Cover with the partly drained tomatoes and wine, season lightly. Cover and cook in a moderate oven for about 45 minutes, or until tender. Remove the lid, cover the veal with cheese and place under a moderate grill until the cheese has melted and lightly browned. Serve at once garnished with herbs.

Cumberland veal

Metric	Imperial
4 veal escalopes, beaten	4 veal escalopes, beaten
Salt and freshly ground black pepper	Salt and freshly ground black pepper
50 g butter	2 oz butter
1 medium-sized onion, peeled and chopped	1 medium-sized onion, peeled and chopped
150 ml port	¼ pint port
4 × 15 ml spoons white stock	4 tablespoons white stock
1 × 15 ml spoon redcurrant jelly	1 tablespoon redcurrant jelly
100 g mushrooms, cleaned, trimmed and sliced	4 oz mushrooms, cleaned, trimmed and sliced
2 × 5 ml spoons lemon juice	2 teaspoons lemon juice
100 ml double cream	4 fl oz double cream
To garnish:	To garnish:
Parsley sprigs (optional)	Parsley sprigs (optional)

Cooking Time: 35–40 minutes.

Trim the veal and season lightly with salt and pepper. Melt the butter in a large frying pan and fry the onion until soft. Add the veal and cook for 2 to 3 minutes each side. Add the port, stock, redcurrant jelly and seasonings and bring to the boil. Add the mushrooms and cover the pan. Simmer gently for 10 to 15 minutes until the veal is tender. Taste and adjust the seasonings and sharpen with lemon juice. Stir in the cream and heat gently to just below boiling point. Serve garnished with parsley sprigs, if liked.

Veal Montmorency

Metric	Imperial
4 veal escalopes, beaten flat, or 4 veal cutlets	4 veal escalopes, beaten flat, or 4 veal cutlets
Salt and freshly ground black pepper	Salt and freshly ground black pepper
25 g butter	1 oz butter
1 × 15 ml spoon oil	1 tablespoon oil
396 g can black cherries	14 oz can black cherries
4 × 15 ml spoons Madeira	4 tablespoons Madeira
2 × 5 ml spoons lemon juice	2 teaspoons lemon juice
150 ml white stock	¼ pint white stock
2 × 5 ml spoons cornflour	2 teaspoons cornflour
To garnish:	To garnish:
Watercress sprigs	Watercress sprigs
Lattice potatoes (optional)	Lattice potatoes (optional)

Cooking Time: 20–45 minutes.

Trim the veal and season lightly on both sides. Heat the butter with the oil in a large frying pan and fry the escalopes for 2 to 3 minutes on each side, or fry the cutlets until browned on both sides. Drain the cherries and add the juice to the pan with the Madeira, lemon juice and stock. Bring to the boil, cover and simmer gently, about 10 minutes for the escalopes and 20 to 25 minutes for the cutlets, or until tender. Skim any fat from the surface of the juices, taste and adjust seasonings. Blend the cornflour with a little cold water and stir into the sauce. Bring to the boil, add the cherries and simmer for a further 5 minutes. Serve garnished with watercress, and lattice potatoes if liked.

Veal Montmorency; Steak Sophia; Cumberland veal; Veal Jessica

Steak Sophia

Metric

8 thin slices fillet steak
2 cloves garlic, crushed
Salt and freshly ground
black pepper
50 g butter
2 × 15 ml spoons finely
chopped onion
2 × 5 ml spoons
Worcestershire sauce
1 × 15 ml spoon lemon
juice
2 × 15 ml spoons finely
chopped parsley
2–4 × 15 ml spoons
brandy
3–4 × 15 ml spoons
double cream

To garnish:
Fried button mushrooms
(optional)

Imperial

8 thin slices fillet steak
2 cloves garlic, crushed
Salt and freshly ground
black pepper
2 oz butter
2 tablespoons finely
chopped onion
2 teaspoons Worcestershire
sauce
1 tablespoon lemon juice
2 tablespoons finely
chopped parsley
2–4 tablespoons brandy
3–4 tablespoons double
cream

To garnish:
Fried button mushrooms
(optional)

Cooking Time: about 15 minutes.

Beat the steaks lightly, rub all over with crushed garlic and season lightly. Melt the butter in a large frying pan and fry the onion until soft. Add the steaks and fry quickly for 1 to 2 minutes on each side. Add the Worcestershire sauce, lemon juice, parsley and seasonings. Ignite the brandy, add to the pan and simmer for 1 to 2 minutes. Stir in the cream and reheat without boiling. Taste and adjust the seasonings and served garnished with mushrooms, if liked.
Note: the cream can be omitted, if preferred.

Index